How to Become a
Stressfree Trader

How to Become a
Stressfree Trader

The Accidental Discoveries of an
Applied Behavioral Science Student

Jason Starzec and Mark Crisp

iUniverse, Inc.
New York Lincoln Shanghai

How to Become a Stressfree Trader
The Accidental Discoveries of an Applied Behavioral Science Student

iUniverse, Inc.

For information address:
iUniverse, Inc.
2021 Pine Lake Road, Suite 100
Lincoln, NE 68512
www.iuniverse.com

ISBN: 0-595-27505-2

Printed in the United States of America

Dedications

I always read dedications that sound something like this, "I wanted to thank my family for allowing me to lock myself in my room for six months in order to complete this book. Thank you for giving me the opportunity to finish this book".

But what I want to know is where in the world do those authors find their families! I couldn't even imagine my family "allowing me to finish" a book! So I also would like to dedicate this book to my family. But instead of thanking them for allowing me to write, I would like to dedicate this book to them *despite* their constant attempts to thwart the finishing of this project! My five year old daughter, my three year old son, and my seven month old son all had very good intentions. But think of the biggest number you can possibly think of. Put that number in your head and hold it there. Now double it, because this is the number of times I heard "Dad, I need your help putting the clothes on this Barbie" and the number of messy diapers I changed while I was writing this book (but not the copy in your hand). So instead of thanking them for allowing me to finish, I would like to tell them that I finished this book despite their efforts to the contrary!

I of course would also like to thank Dr. Maria Malayter, whose inspirations for the material in this book were at times subtle, sometimes accidental, and always profound. Positive energy has a wonderful way of manifesting itself in those close to the source.

Likewise, I realize that it goes without saying but without the guidance, extraordinary trading strategies, and investment tutelage of Mark Crisp this book never would have happened. Hopefully now many more people will get the opportunity to thank Mr. Crisp for giving them something nobody else has: THE POWER TO TRADE FOR THEMSELVES!!

And I can't write about acknowledgements without saying thanks to my wife who is successful enough so that I can stay home and write books and fix Barbie's clothes and think about all the money she is making for me to invest!

Contents

Introduction

The old saying tells us that a faulty craftsman blames his tools. So is it reasonable to assume that a faulty trader blames the market? Absolutely!

You positively will not see a successful trader out there who does not take full responsibility for his investment actions and reactions. The truly successful trader has accepted (and even thrived upon) every decision that needs to be made, every action that requires a response, and every problem that demands a solution. There are no excuses. He just couldn't have it any other way.

What is the first thing that comes to your mind when you think of the term "stressfree trading"? Some of you might be thinking about low risk (low yield!) trading that allows you to focus on the rest of your life because you know that your portfolio can yield no lower than 2.5% and no higher than 3.5%. You can rest easy because you don't have to put any thought into your money at all. There is no checking the newspaper in the morning to see whether or not you are going to have a good day or a bad day. You can simply coast through your days knowing that your "investment" is completely FDIC insured and there is no possibility of losing your money. You are stress free.

Others of you may think of "stressfree trading" as simply an attitude and that there are just some people who are meant to trade and invest while others are not because they get nervous at merely the hint of the word "risk". You may think that some people just can't handle the normal stresses of investing and really shouldn't be involved with it in the first place. In other words, those who invest have accepted the fact that there will be an average amount of stress no matter how you trade. They have accepted the fact that Pepto Bismol will be on their grocery list each week. It's just a part of life. The acceptance of this normalcy of investment stress makes stress predictable…and therefore manageable.

And there are still others who believe that there could be no such thing as "stressfree trading"; that the term itself is an oxymoron. How could something that is innately and universally stressful ever be "stressfree"?

So the ultimate question becomes, "What is stressfree trading?" or perhaps more importantly, "How do I achieve stressfree trading?" The answer is amazingly simple in an investment world that is exceedingly complicated. Behind all the numbers, behind all the facts, behind all the charts and lists and graphs and explanations and promises there lies a system. There is always a system behind any process. A nutritionalist may tell someone who is overweight that they need to eat fewer calories and exercise more. The nutritionalist will show plenty of charts and graphs that show exactly what can happen to a person who continues to be overweight. That nutritionalist will also give plenty of reasons and explanations for why the individual is overweight. There may be mitigating circumstances that are seemingly beyond control. There may be risks. There may be rewards. But no matter what, the solution lies within the system. There must be a system of change in order to produce the desired result. The individual will need to, on some level, change the way he or she goes about their daily routine. Changes to their system, their life, must be made. The system includes all the actions, all the thoughts, all the words that make up that individual. If that individual wants to change something, he or she must first change the system.

Think about it for a minute. If something is going poorly or not meeting expectations then something has to change. If investors lose money and feel that their portfolio is not producing the desired results, then something must change…or else the results will remain the same indefinitely (save for the occasional lucky person who does everything wrong and still comes out on top, like Carrottop or Bob Saget!). And what exactly has to change? The system! All the attitudes, all the trades, all the "gut feelings", all the withdrawals, all the deposits, all that and everything else makes up an investor's system of investing. And if the results are not good, then the system must change!

But I'll go one step further. If the results are not *perfect*, then the system must change! Something must be changed or tweaked or slightly altered if you are not getting the absolute most you can possibly be getting out of your investments. If you are not 100% thrilled with the way your portfolio looks then it would only make sense that something can be changed in order to maximize your earnings and ultimately your happiness! But how do you change your system? How do you change your way of life? For me it happened by accident, I got lucky…

When I first entered Maria's Applied Behavioral Science class at National-Louis University near Chicago, I could just tell that things were about to change. There was a positive aura that consumed the class like none I had felt before. I just had no idea that what was about to seriously change in my life was the way I looked at investing! I doubt that anybody goes through an Applied Behavioral Science program so that they can become better investors. And believe me, the program was not designed to teach students how to become better investors. It (luckily) just happened that way!

This book tells the story about a student (a student in all senses of the word) who meets an Applied Behavioral Science teacher named Maria and learns more about investing and finance and the way money works in the world today than he could have ever hoped for. This is especially noteworthy because it happened in a class that had nothing to do with investments or finance or money at all...except maybe that the cost of the class was itself a lesson in finance!

Not only did I learn the underlying habits, motivations, and thought processes of highly successful traders, I also learned exact trading methods that come as close to "stressfree trading" as any I had ever seen.

I would very much like to pass that experience and that extraordinary information along to you. Thank you for that opportunity!

Section I

The Seven Secrets of the Successful Trader

1

Good Karma

I was amazed to find out exactly what can be learned in a college Adult Behavior and Applied Behavioral Science class. At first it certainly sounded as though I would learn a great deal about how to talk to others in an adult and professional manner. Perhaps I would learn some of the differences between adults and children. Whatever it was that I stood to learn, the one sad truth is that that was the first time I really realized that I was an adult (the only child in an adult learning class just didn't seem as feasible as it may have a few years ago)!

It all started innocently enough. All the students sat down in the chairs that were arranged in a circle so that everybody could face and see everybody else. For a while we just looked at each other. The teacher hadn't arrived yet and we weren't quite sure what we were supposed to do or what we were to expect. Eventually, several of the adults began to talk to each other. Do you have any kids? How long did it take you to drive here? Why are you going to school at age 55? The simple kind of talk that adults seem to crave and employers seem to cringe at.

After about thirty minutes we all started to get a little uneasy. We started to openly question whether or not we were in the right classroom. Had the teacher sent us all an email that we just missed? Did the class really start the next week? How long should we wait until we go home?

Then Maria (who we all found out had no children and drove 45 minutes to get to class) decided to stand up. At first I thought for sure she was going to be the first person to leave the classroom. She was going to say, "I've had it with this class today. If the teacher wants to be an hour late that's fine but I have better things to do with my time than sit here and wait for a teacher to show up for class!"

To all of our shock (and none of yours if you read the introduction!), she announced that she was the instructor for this Applied Behavioral Science class. It was an old trick. She simply wanted to show us how easy it is for humans to communicate. It is in our nature to get together with each other and talk about things that either are important (like children and money) as well as things that aren't so important (like what kind of car we would like to drive if our spouses would let us). Adult communication is an innate characteristic of humans. We like to talk! That is one of our universal behaviors.

She went on to explain that she was going to run this class a little differently than we may have expected. By this point that was inevitable! She didn't exactly tell us how she was going to instruct the class but she wanted to make sure that we were prepared to have an open mind. She also wanted to make sure that we understood that Applied Behavioral Science is a rather broad subject. The goal of the class and the entire college program was to integrate the knowledge gained in the educational sources into our own lives. We were to analyze and ultimately improve our life systems!

For instance, if Maria were to tell us that she wanted us all to get in a group and talk about the items that would be most important if we were stranded in a desert, then we should truly believe that we were stranded in a desert. We should totally remove ourselves from ourselves if only for a moment in order to maximize the learning potential. Total displacement.

She then told us why she doesn't drink caffeine anymore because of the dangers caffeine poses to our body and mind. At that point we were all given a fond farewell and were allowed to go home early. So I drank the rest of my coffee, packed up my books that had gone completely unused during that first session, and ran to my car while quite eager to get home in time to catch the rest of Monday Night Football!

2
Total Responsibility

The first thing that Maria said to us as we all sat down for our next class was, "Please close your eyes".

This was no problem since I had only begun my first cup of coffee for the evening. Unfortunately, she continued: "Imagine you get a call from a hotshot publisher who wants to send a writer to your home and interview you. This writer is going to write a bibliography of you. The book about your life will be published. Imagine that this writer sits down in your living room with a tape recorder and a laptop computer and asks you one simple question. The writer asks you to explain yourself."

At first I thought this would be an extremely easy task to accomplish. After all, I really didn't have much problem sipping my coffee even if my eyes were closed! But I thought long and I thought hard. It was a rather complex assignment but it was an interesting one and one that warranted my cooperation. I started imagining that I would tell this writer about all my proudest moments as a father, a teacher, a writer, and an investor. I began to imagine who I wanted to become when all of a sudden Maria said to the class, "And now I want you to do the same thing…but this time be totally honest. What *are* you going to say to that bibliographer? How are you going to really explain yourself?"

This new task, although not as fun, was certainly more challenging. I began to make small changes to my story from moments before. I changed "I was so proud of my son when he broke Hank Aaron's career home run record" to "I was so proud of my son when he graduated college. I'm so happy that he found happiness and meaning in his life".

I then began to think proactively. In other words, I started envisioning my future. I envisioned my goals, my wants, my needs, my life before it had been lived. We learned that this little trick of envisioning your future in a hypothetical yet realistic way turned out to be Stephen Covey's First Habit of proactivity (Covey, 1989, pgs. 66–71). Now, I was thinking probably the same thing that you are thinking about proactivity. That means to take the initiative, right?

But Covey explains that proactivity may not mean only what you are thinking that it means. In fact, as I notice that the word proactivity continues to be underlined in red by my computer, the word is not even accepted in the standard dictionary of the English language. Of course like I said before and especially if you work in the corporate world, I'm sure that you understand the word to mean initiative. Doing things before they need to be done. Action before necessity. (Covey, pg.71). But I learned that proactivity means so much more than taking the initiative at work or in your church group or with your family. What I learned in the class is that, simply put, proactivity means that "as human beings, we are responsible for our own lives" (Covey, pg. 71).

Those words kept echoing in my mind: We are responsible for our own lives. We are responsible. We are completely responsible. There are no excuses. There is nobody to blame for what happens to us. We choose our destinies and we choose the paths we take. Wow, no wonder that book sold 18 billion copies, and that was only the first habit!

Now I'm not sure if it was the four cups of coffee that I drank during class or the incredibly provocative discussions throughout the session but I never had a more riveting drive than that drive home *after* that class! I simply could not stop thinking about the issues that were discussed. I was mesmerized. I had a conversation with myself that reminded me of a political debate that you may see on television. I argued with myself. I objected to myself. I couldn't stop talking about what had transpired.

So naturally when I got home I immediately ran to my wife and began to revisit the topics discussed in class. I went on and on about Covey's principle until I noticed that my wife was rubbing her forehead. Her only response to my informative and invocative words was, "For goodness sake, can you please just turn off the lights and let me sleep!"

Well, I knew that I couldn't simply plop into bed and peacefully drift into a deep sleep. That is when I remembered my Blue's Clues (this reference will also help to keep the attention of any toddlers that may be reading this book)! My daughter calls it Dad's Thinking Time when I sit down in my Thinking Chair every so often and just Think, Think, Think…

I thought of the usefulness of what I had learned. I thought about the implications of this new knowledge. And of course, I thought about how this new knowledge could help me financially (the investment nerd that I am—most discussions with myself end up with, "Now how can this help my portfolio?").

What I realized is that a successful trader never blames anybody or anything. He knows every single action he takes. This is the first major secret of the successful trader. You will never meet a successful trader who is looking to blame someone or something else for the consequences of his results. You just won't see it because a successful trader takes pride in accepting his decisions. He *wants* to be responsible!

You see, when you accept 100% of the responsibility for your actions with no questions asked then you close the door to excuses behind you. For the unsuccessful trader (and the unsuccessful person for that matter), there is far too much time being spent trying to find out who is to blame or what is to blame. Did the market go down? Did oil prices go up? What could have possibly happened that I had no control over to make things turn out so bad? The successful trader, on the other hand, will accept responsibility when something goes wrong and vow that he will never make the same mistake again. He will not spend valuable time and energy trying to find excuses or someone else to blame. That time should be spent examining the problem, noting it, discovering a solution, and moving on! Simply put, you should be willing to accept the fact that you will occasionally make a mistake. You will occasionally make the wrong decision. Mistakes are inevitable. You can't avoid them completely. So make the most of them and turn it around in your favor. Give yourself the edge you have been looking for, the edge you need to succeed. Take the opportunity to learn. Learn when others are busy trying to make excuses.

And most importantly, **don't repeat the mistake**!

Now think for one moment. Why do you believe that taking responsibility for your actions is so important? Is it to be a stand-up guy? Is it so that you can be happy with yourself knowing that you are doing the *right* thing? Maybe. But I'm all for finding what helps my portfolio. And taking full responsibility for my actions will help my portfolio. It will help my future and it is what has helped ALL the most successful traders out there today. And that is why I don't make any excuses. That is why I won't spend one second trying to find a reason for failure that was beyond my control. Because one thing is for sure: You will never learn from your mistakes if you don't first admit that you made a mistake! You will simply make the mistake, convince yourself that it was someone else's fault, and then make the same mistake in a different situation just because you switched brokers! Trust me, it's not his or her fault…it's yours. And the sooner you truly believe that the sooner you can start learning from your mistakes. This is an absolutely vital component of any winning trader's system.

Could you imagine Warren Buffet losing a few million dollars on a share trade and them blaming the general conditions of the market? Or blaming his broker for giving him dud advice?! No way! It's just not going to happen because the first thing that winning traders do when something goes wrong is ask themselves, "Did I follow my rules?"[1]

If the answer is "yes" then they will look long and hard at their rules to make sure that they have the right system. Is there something that could be changed in their rules to avoid making this mistake again? Probably not. But it is quite important to ask this first because if the answer turns out to be "no" then there needs to be some deep personal evaluation and explanation. The trader will really have to dig deep to understand why he didn't follow his rules. Was I afraid? Was there some mitigating circumstance? Is it possible for me to not follow my rules again? What can I do to change this behavior, or am I just not comfortable with my rules?[2]

But do you happen to notice the one common with all of these questions? "How can I…" "Why did I…" "Will I…"

---

1.   Don't worry, you'll read a lot more about your rules in the following chapters!
2.   For more on systems and choosing the rules that fit you, sit tight! It's just ahead in Chapter Three.

In these situations the trader is taking full responsibility for his actions. He fully realizes that it is up to him to understand what he needs to change in order to be successful. What does he need to tweak? He is basically reiterating to himself the fact that he is in charge. It wasn't his broker. It wasn't the market. He needs to make the change. He needs to make it right.

If you have to ask, you shouldn't be trading.

Have you ever heard that before? It is an old saying in the world of trading (and I imagine many other endeavors as well). But take a look at that statement in the world of trading. If you have a sound system that you have tested and proven over the long run and you know darn well that the system is perfect for you and it has outperformed the market over time and will continue to do so…then why should you EVER have to ask for someone else's opinion? Don't be swayed by the doubting Thomases of the world. If your system has proven itself time and time again then what possible good could a third person opinion provide (apart from confusing you and clouding your judgement)?

If your first lesson was to take responsibility for ALL of your actions then the next logical lesson is to stay true to what you believe. If you are a long term trend follower then why ask the opinion of a day trader? If you are a value investor then the opinions of a momentum trader will be a complete waste of time. No two people have the same opinion. And it is likely that nobody else will have your system of trading. So don't start believing someone else just because they have an opinion. Stick to your rules. Take responsibility and make it all yours.

Thirdly, don't be like everybody else. It seems that so many people want to be told how to trade. They want to be told how to be successful. You need to tell yourself right now that you need to act on your own. You need to make your success. Mark McGwire can't tell you how to hit a home run. That information would be useless to you.

Bobby Fisher can't tell you how to win at chess. If you don't need it, then don't ask! Don't ask Michael Jordan how he could dunk so well in the hopes that you may be able to pick up enough inside information to perform a 360 degree slam. It just doesn't work that way. You have to play to *your* strengths. You have to make your success.

You can't be told how to be successful from someone else. This is one of the major reasons why people fail in the markets today. They don't accept the work themselves. They think someone else can simply tell them how to start a successful online casino business and then they apply that knowledge and rake in millions. If you don't take responsibility for yourself then you will just be playing someone else's game. You may even make *them* rich!

Of course, I certainly do not imply that there is nothing out there to learn from other people. I just mean you have to be selective about who you learn from. If the information is irrelevant, then don't waste your time. Don't ask a baseball player how to play chess. Stick to your strengths!

Now, if you ever find yourself wanting to ask a third party about your position or why your position didn't work then remember these simple rules:

- Close the position out (uncertainty in yourself is no way to trade)

- Review your plan and rules

- Work out why you lack the responsibility to follow your plan (conquer your fears)

- When you are convinced that you don't need a third party opinion then you have regained your responsibility and you can start trading again

This is all well and good for those of you who know exactly what to do to gain responsibility for your trades (or for those who already have). But most of us need to know where to begin (I certainly pondered that question for quite some time)! But how exactly can a trader learn to accept total responsibility?

The first thing you have to do is design a set of rules and realize THE most important point in trading is following those rules to a tee. And never sway from those rules because you know that you put forth the time and effort to make those rules perfect (it is important to make the rules so perfect for you that you have total confidence in them…it's not going to do you much good if you constantly are questioning the value of your rules).

Once you have a set of firmly established rules then you will find that you will have very little use for outside opinion. In fact, I go to great lengths to completely avoid outside opinions! I am confident in my rules and I have taken complete responsibility for all of my trades. I don't give myself any option to make excuses. If I listen to nobody but myself then I can't possibly blame anybody *but* myself! I have made my rules work. And once my rules have been put to the test, I have realized that they produce great results. I now am on the right side of the market about 95% of the time. Had I listened to outside opinions along the way, it would have taken me so much longer to reach the successful point that I am at today. With a hundred detours comes a longer travel time. You all know that the shortest distance between two points is a straight line, right? And believe me, the figures I now get with my rules is much better than *any* outside source can offer. That ought to be your goal as well. Get to the point that your rules produce results that are better than any outside advice can produce. That way you will ultimately lose any temptation at all to listen to other opinions.

So from this point forward, begin to learn what it takes to accept full responsibility for your trades and all of your trading decisions. It will be so much easier and quicker to narrow your path towards success if you only have one person and one set of rules that you are dealing with.

Think of it like this. Let's say you have one hundred marbles of different colors but only one of the marbles is green. You need to sift through your bag of marbles one by one until you reach the green one (we all want the green one). It may take a while. After all, one green marble in a bag of one hundred different marbles is kind of like a needle in a haystack. But it's manageable. You know that if you eliminate marbles one by one then you will eventually reach the green marble.

Now pretend that you get ten emails and ten phone calls from marble experts. They all have their bag of marbles and insist that you do things their way. They can help you find your green marble if you would just take a look at their bag of marbles. They can give you information. They can give you advice. They can give you more marbles. So you accept one of their offers. That "expert" then dumps his bag of marbles into yours. Well, that didn't work but you still take the marbles out one by one in the hopes of finding your one green marble. Now other "experts" continue to dump their bag of marbles into yours. All the while you are sorting the marbles in your bag one by one to try and find the coveted green one.

Now, it is possible that you may get lucky and find your green marble. But can you see that you are going the wrong way? Instead of eliminating the bad marbles and increasing your chances of success, you keep adding more bad marbles and decreasing your odds of winning.

So start eliminating your bad marbles and don't let others add their bad marbles to your mix. If you stick with yours, it may take a while but your chances for success will improve each and every day. You will start out with a one out of a hundred chance. Then you won't find what you are looking for so you eliminate one bad idea. Now you have a one in a ninety-nine chance of success. Eventually, if you continue down this path then success will become inevitable. Your chances will, one day, be one out of one. You will have no choice but to succeed. So don't let others add their bad marbles to your bag…don't let your odds to go from one out of 37 to one out of 237…do you?!

Don't lose sight of your rules. Keep following them and making them your own because you will soon realize the importance of keeping to your rules and not changing them because of the advice of others. Following those rules will ultimately determine whether or not you win or lose in the long run.

And if you ever find yourself thinking, "They did this" or "The market caused that loss" make sure you instantly change those thoughts to "Did I follow my rules?"

If the answer is "yes" then pat yourself on the back because you are well on your way to becoming a market winner (one in the minority). If the answer is "no" then ask yourself why you broke your rules. Why did you not take full responsibility? Will you do that again? Make sure the answer to that last question is a resounding "NO"!

3

Have a System That Fits You

Little did I know when I entered my second class that I would learn more about temperament and personality than I ever would wish upon anybody! In fact, I felt as though I was losing a small part of *my* personality by learning so much about everyone else's. The class started simply enough when we were asked by Maria to take the Keirsey (1984) "Temperament Sorter" in order to determine what temperament type we were.

The explanation was simple: In order to effectively communicate with others and paint an accurate picture of the other person, you must first know yourself by accurately painting a picture of yourself (Keirsey, 1984, pg. 4). But more importantly, what I learned that day is that if I am able to fully understand who I am as a person and appreciate what makes me tick then I can apply that knowledge to situations in my life. As a result, I will better understand what it is I need to do to make the best of a situation. I will know what makes me happy and what makes me comfortable. I will become comfortable with my decisions if I know exactly why I made those decisions and why those decisions are important to me.

Of course, I didn't immediately see the connection between discovering myself and making gains in the stock market but it sure was extremely fascinating for me to find out about me! And everybody else in the class felt the same way. Archie, who was sitting two chairs over, exclaimed that he never knew that he was so goal-oriented. Cindy on the other side of the room said that she finally realized why her and her husband can't reach common ground on what color to paint the living room. It was as if a light was turned on where once there had been dark. We all had revelations!

What I found out about myself (other than the fact that I belong to a group of personality types that is found in only one percent of the population!) is that I am rather self confident and I truly believe that if there is a task to be done it would never be so big or so difficult that I couldn't do it (this may be why I have gotten into hour long discussions with my six-year old on how to fix a Barbie doll that had been chewed in half by the dog). I also found out that my temperament (INTJ) suggests that I am always open for suggestions and that I am constantly trying to find the best way to get things done (Keirsey, pg. 180). I am always trying to figure out and manipulate things in order to make it work for me, yet I am devoted to the world of numbers (Keirsey, pg. 181). Funny, it seems as though I want to take something as concrete as mathematics and somehow manipulate the numbers so that I always come out on top.

That class seemed to provide an overdue key to the locked doors of my personality and what makes the world around me work for *me*. I learned who I was and I learned what systems worked for me (and why they worked).

The minutes began to drag as I thought about how I could best apply this new information. The gears upstairs were churning like never before because I knew that I was truly on to something. Once I knew who I was as a person and what made me comfortable, I would no longer be afraid of the decisions that needed to be made. I could concentrate on the solutions to problems instead of the problems themselves. I wouldn't have to spend time thinking about how best to do something…but rather I would easily conclude what was the *only* way to do something!

Of course, when I got home that night I had to sit down in my Thinking Chair and review the day's (life's) lessons. What did it mean to really know myself? What did it mean to really know who I was? What did it mean to be comfortable with myself? And how could I translate that into success as an investor?!

The most important lesson that I learned about investing that day was that every investor, every money manager, every trader, every *person* has a system that fits them. Some are long term, some are mechanical, and some are intuitive. Some systems are purely mathematical and some are purely based in emotion and what "feels" right.

Whatever the person is; whether it be a day trader, a momentum trader, a value trader, an index trader, a scalper; it doesn't matter. Because you could find at least one person in the world who is successful at each of these systems of trading. There is always going to be someone out there that made trading used toothbrushes work! With every system I give you, you could give me a list of winners and losers who have used that system. Clearly, then, it can't possibly be because of the system itself. So what is it?

I learned in class that none of the answers to the Keirsey temperament sorter are right or wrong. In fact, almost every question is answered "yes" by half of the American population and "no" by the other half (Keirsey, pg. 4). So what makes the test so special?

In case you didn't guess already, it's the combination that is unique. Some people will answer "yes" to some of the questions and "no" to other questions. When it is all said and done, each person will have a sort of "score" at the end. No single answer was more important than another. But the combination of answers is what makes the person. Those answers indicate what is important to the person, what makes that unique individual tick. They reveal what makes that person comfortable. (Keirsey, pgs. 13–19)

And so it is with trading. It's not the answers that count. It's not the individual preferences. It's not the system. But rather it's the system that fits the personality. Investors need to choose the system that makes them comfortable. They need to choose a system that won't make them lose sleep. They need to feel good about the decisions they make. Momentum trading is for some but not for others. Some like day trading. Some are only comfortable buying government bonds. The point is that the successful trader needs to find the system that fits them the best.

Let me reiterate: The system does not matter. The only thing that matters is the *right* system. I've heard of value investors (of which Warren Buffet is one) who make millions and millions from the stock market. I've heard of day traders taking home over $2 million a year in profits. I've heard of a dancer who makes $2.5 million a year momentum trading on the side. What do you think they all have in common? Certainly not the system because they are all using a different one. No, they have simply chosen a system that they are comfortable with and that they happen to excel at. They operate a style of trading that puts them at ease. They do not stress about their decisions because they know that those decisions are coming from them. No one told them to trade this way. They just discovered the combination on their own. They may not have even known that they were doing it. They may have gotten lucky by choosing the style that fits them the best. Well, you can't exactly count on luck in this game, can you? No way, you don't have to be lucky! You now have the knowledge. You can go out and find the system that works best for you.[1]

But one thing I learned from my class was that things tended to sound better when they come from other people. I'm sure you have seen a million commercials on television and a million (or more) spam emails telling how much money this person or that person has made doing the latest get-rich-quick scheme. Too many traders try to copy the latest hot fad in trading. The biggest fad right now is day trading. Now I am certainly not saying that day trading does not work. As I said before, there are many day traders out there who have made plenty of money day trading. But that style of trading just won't suit everyone. To be a successful day trader you have to love the short term ups and downs of the market. You have to feel energized and excited when there is activity. You have to feel good about the lows because you know you are due for some highs.

Sure, there are plenty of day traders out there making money in day trading. But chances are, they are either meant to be day traders because that style of constant up and down activity suits them just fine…or they are getting treated for ulcers every other week. It's a lot like Keirsey's extravert, you have to feel energized by the environment around you (your external environment). Day trading for some people is like a constant party. The music is blaring, people are talking and dancing, the television in on in the background, and there's confetti everywhere. Some people just love this, they feed off the energy in the room and when the party is over they go home and talk about it for a couple hours before going to bed. If the party were day trading, then those energized people who want to leave one party to go to another would be perfectly suited for day trading! They'd probably love it![2]

---

1.   Although you may not want to run out and immediately find your system to use…you may want to finish this book first because there is a lot more to it!

2.   It must be said that I have not analyzed which temperaments belong to which types of trading…I am merely pointing out that day trading seems an awful lot like that party that keeps on going and if you really like that kind of activity and that constant excitement then day trading may suit you just fine.

In other words, even though some succeed, there are plenty out there who have lost their shirts (and their minds) within a couple of months and have to get out of the market before they can truly know whether or not day trading fits their temperament!

Likewise, there are some traders who would find it quite torturous to buy a stock and hold on to it for a year. Although long term investing can offer fantastic rewards with very little work (good things to those who wait), those who do not possess the patience and discipline that long term investing requires will get frustrated and fail for lack of trying. Those people who cannot wait are obviously not suited for long term investing. Those who have a great deal of patience and who have no problems "riding it out" all the way to the top are those who may be best suited for long term investing.

You can imagine that choosing a system or a trading personality may be like choosing a career. I remember reading a book some time ago about the world's greatest managers. One thing that the author made sure to emphasize time and time again was that these top managers and overachievers absolutely LOVED their careers. They loved going to work. They loved the challenge. Most of them said that they couldn't believe that they got paid to do what they naturally loved to do. But do you really think it has anything to do with the career itself? Of course not. I could easily find a nurse who loved more than anything in the world being a nurse. That nurse would rise out of bed each day so looking forward to spending the day in the hospital and helping people. She yearned for it. She loved her job. On the other hand, I could easily find a nurse who hated her job. She hated having to constantly be looking after sick people all day long. She hated having to change diapers for a living. She thought her paycheck was far too small for the sacrifices she had to make. It's not the job. It's not the career. It's the match that counts! And it's the same thing with trading.

You will find that you will only be able to be a top trader if you find the trading system that you love and that you really believe in for yourself. You wouldn't swap that trading method for anything. No matter what fads come along that promise millions within weeks. No matter what your friends think or how they trade. You will have that much better of a chance to excel at this system of trading because your heart will be in it. And the profits that will naturally come will just be icing on the cake!

Now, realizing that this is what you have to do may be the easy part or it may be the hard part (perhaps it depends on your temperament type…you can consult with the Keirsey books on this one!). But no matter if it is the hardest thing for you to do or the easiest thing, realizing what it is you need to do is most certainly the *first* thing you need to do. The next part is finding the system that you are happiest with. How do you do that? I have found that it helps to work backwards. First work out your objectives! What is it that you need to accomplish? What is it that you *can* accomplish based on what you know of yourself?

Ask these specific questions of yourself and your goals, and for goodness sake, be honest:

- What annual rate of return do I want?

- Do I want to trade full time, part time, or hardly any time?

- Can I handle the stress of day trading and short term trading?

- Do I have the patience for long term trading?

- What kind of personality am I (do I need lots of action, do I need to make decisions all the time, do I need to occasionally take a break from trading, etc.)?

- What trading books have I read and which top traders do I most admire and why?

- Could I easily copy the methods and styles of these traders?

Whatever you do, make sure that you don't fixate on those last two questions. Don't run out and try to copy a hotshot day trader if you find that day trading is not exactly for you. Those last two questions should help you understand what your long term goals are. Find the successes and study how they became successes. Then strive to find the method of trading that best fits you as a trader and a person. Find which method you will be most comfortable with and aim to become even better at that method then those you emulate. Try to be the best at the method you are best at!

I personally like the thought of buying a share at $30 and selling it nine months later for $130. Sure I can't expect it to happen every time. But wouldn't it be great for it to just happen a few times a year? Wouldn't that make me happy? Wouldn't I think that was a wonderful decision and a great return? Yes…but that's me! I am very patient and work hard to trade the way that suits me best. This same scenario would just about kill the prototypical day trader.

"What do you mean it hasn't risen to my goal in six hours? This is terrible…where's the Pepto Bismol?!"

I, however, see absolutely nothing wrong with sitting on the sidelines for a couple of months. If the conditions aren't right for me than I will not trade. I love the idea of spending just a few minutes per day checking the charts and the rest of the time is mine to study and write and learn and teach. For me the big money is in the big moves, not the individual fluctuations.

Waiting around for the big score. This will certainly not suit every-one! But the point is that after many years of trial and error and trying to find what fits me the most and the method I'm most comfortable with, I have found the system that is absolutely perfect for me. And I aim to become THE world's best trader with this system.[3] You must do the same, and it sure doesn't have to be with one of the systems that I will tell you about later.

After all, if you are trading a system that does not fit your exact per-sonality and comfort levels then you can never gain the confidence you need to succeed. And without that confidence, you will have to get lucky in order to see the results we are all looking for; the results that translate into truly large profits. And who wants to rely on luck?

So to make a long story short, if you are a new trader or an unsuc-cessful one then I urge you to ask yourself: What kind of trading style or method best suits my personality?[4] Since this is the foundation for success in trading then make sure you spend a great deal of time inves-tigating this point. Get this right because if you don't then you will have a far greater chance of failure even if the system seems to be "the best one out there today". So build a strong foundation and your trad-ing system will be strong and stand the test of time. On the contrary, build a weak foundation and your trading system will crumble (along with your money).

Unfortunately, this is where a majority of the traders go wrong today. They have no idea which style of trading suits them the best. They spend so much time trying to find the best trading system or the best trading method that they fail to realize what trading system is best

---

3.   For more on the specific systems of trading that I am talking about…please be patient! You will read about them in section II.
4.   If you need help determining your personality, you may want to check out Keirsey's *Please Understand Me: Character and Temperament Types*

for them. They keep buying into the latest fad or the latest software. They keep listening to the new trading guru on the block hoping that this will change their trading results (or perhaps their trading luck). Most never get to know what successful trading is all about. Did you know that the average trader only lasts SIX MONTHS?! This means that most traders are out of the market before they even get an opportunity to figure out how they should be trading and what methods they should be using. They focused too much of their time, energy, and money on trading the best system when they should have been taking note of what system (or pieces of systems) is best for them.

I firmly believe that any trader who can last over two years in the market will probably go on to become one of those rare breeds: A Stock Market Winner. Why? Because if they have lasted that long then they have began to understand and develop a sense of what works for them. Luck can only take traders so far. Although there are the rare lottery winners out there, good luck for most traders does not last long. In order for them to have any stability in the market and any endurance, they will need to at least begin to recognize and develop the system that is best for them. They'll need to start trading in a way that they are comfortable with. I don't know many people who can last more than two years with ulcers from trading induced stress. Two years of success seems to indicate that the trader has found their niche. Think about it. Most traders will never get two years of experience before they lose their money and/or their interest and/or their sanity.

Say it today and say it often:

"I will find a system that fits me and I will become THE world's best trader at this one style of trading…at my style of trading."

When I thought more and more about what I had learned in class about temperament types and trying to figure out my own temperament and personality so that I could more effectively communicate with myself and with others, my investment strategy really started to show itself. It was quite clear that I needed to figure out what works for me, what my investment temperament is, in order to be comfortable enough with my investments to really make a difference. I needed to really search myself. I needed to find who I was as an investor, as a trader. But most importantly, I knew that I needed to begin. I needed to commit. Once that was accomplished, my investment path seemed that much less treacherous.

So get to work! There is a lot of soul searching that will need to be done.

4

Plan a Trade and Trade a Plan

Even though the next class was only a week away, it seemed as though I had waited months to get back there (and I always thought that I didn't care for school!). I knew that I had an awful lot to think about and could probably fill a few months with what I felt I needed to accomplish up to that point. But I was awfully eager to find out what we were going to learn next!

When I entered the class (just a little late due to the babysitter's late arrival), all the other classmates were lined up against the wall according to height. I went to the appropriate position and stood between someone who was slightly taller than me and someone who was slightly shorter. I wasn't sure what the exercise was all about so I asked the person in front of me.

"You know she doesn't tell us anything!" was the reply I received. Evidently, Maria had given just the one order: stand against the wall according to height. We stood there for a while until it was clear that everybody who was going to make it to class was already there. Then Maria told us to be quiet and listen for a briefing. We were all employees at a large company and she was our new boss. She made it clear that she was a little disappointed with our sales performance. She also made it clear that the owners of the company were also not too happy. They hired Maria to clean things up, to get results. We were then to count off in fours to determine our project groups. Our assignment was to figure out a way to sell one of the company's products. You see, this product that was one of the oldest and most reliable in the company's history, was lagging in sales. People just weren't interested in the product anymore. People were getting bored of it. It was up to us to figure out how to bring this product back from the brink. How to make this product a top seller again. How to get people interested in the product again, even excited about it.

We were ordered to think creatively but effectively. It would be vital to create plans that could be implemented immediately. Organization and efficiency was the key since the owners of the company wanted an answer and wanted it yesterday.

Maria then left the room and returned with the product that we had to save. The product that needed a total marketing overhaul. The product that was going to bring this company to the forefront of consumer sales. So Maria walked back into the room carrying a big, pink hoola-hoop. She set it down on the table, told us she'd be back to get our full reports in fifteen minutes, and left the room. She then poked her head back in the room and said, "Oh, yeah, one more thing. I will examine your results and choose the groups that demonstrated to me their ability to effectively save this product; those groups shall manage this project while the rest of you will find a pink slip in your mailbox by the end of the week".

Well, we knew we didn't have much time so we quickly got into our groups and began to discuss our marketing options. Other than the impending threat over our heads, it was great. Ideas were flying out of people's mouths like they were trying to save the world! We had domestic uses, party uses, high school and college uses, different colors, different sizes, different sounds, and so much more for this little hoola-hoop. We even wrote up a plan to affix soap all the way around the hoola-hoop and market the product to mothers out there.

"Hey, make bathtime for your kids funtime!"

We were in a frenzy to make this the hottest selling product of all time. We jotted down just about everything we could think of and appointed a speaker for our group. We knew there was so much we could do if only there were more time but before we could even think about it, Maria entered the room.

"Time's up", she said. She then ordered us to return to our original chairs and prepare to discuss our results. We were assigned to go first and basically blurted out all the different ways we could market the product. The rest of the groups did pretty much the same thing, and several of our ideas were similar to those of other groups. Maria sat there and patiently listened. I could tell that she thought that some of the ideas were pretty good. I could also tell that she was rather disappointed.

When all the groups had finished presenting their marketing plans, Maria thanked us for our ideas and told us to expect to find pink slips in all of our mailboxes.

"Wait", she said. "Maybe I'll try to avoid using all of my pink paper by showing you a little chart". She flipped open the flipchart to reveal a rather simple organizational drawing. What she had drawn on the flipchart was a traditional organizational chart that she was using to illustrate Cheryl Hamilton's (1997, pg. 45) "formal patterns of relationships and roles needed to get tasks accomplished". She explained to us that the organizational structure is vital in business because it presents a clear and concise plan. This plan could then be used to solve many problems within the company. As long as the company has a reliable and effective plan for solving problems, then project management becomes extremely efficient.

She went on to explain Hamilton's (pg. 45) idea of "division of labor", which is essentially the way in which the organization divides the tasks that need to be accomplished in order to complete a task or a project. The structure that makes this division of labor work is what is widely known as the chain of command. In other words, if there is a task to be completed then the project manager needs to divide up all the subtasks involved and assign them to those employees that (s)he feels would be best suited to effectively and efficiently complete those subtasks (Hamilton, pg. 45). It's all in the system. It's all in the organization. It's all in the plan. Every company has the resource of their people but not every company has the right plan to effectively utilize such a valuable resource.

After Maria enlightened us on what we did wrong and why we really didn't accomplish much of anything (other than take a problem and give it hundreds of potential solutions), she ordered us to regroup and complete the task one more time with the information that we had learned. But before we did that she reminded us of one more piece of advice: Begin with the end in mind. The plan needed to lead us somewhere. It needed to lead us to the end. And we needed to know what the end is if we were to figure out how to get there. Imagine going on vacation and not knowing where you are going. You bought open-ended airline tickets. You packed. You checked the stove. You are all excited but you get to the airport and have no idea what to do next. The plan failed because you did not begin with your destination. So we needed to "begin with the end in mind" (Covey, pg. 97). We needed an organization and a plan. And most importantly, we needed to stick to that plan and implement it exactly as it had been laid out.

When we got back into our groups I felt as though we had discovered something as illuminating and life-altering as how to travel at the speed of light. We quickly realized that I had the most experience as a manager so I was elected to manage the project. I then took our ideas that we had written down and determined what it would take to come up with an effective marketing strategy. I decided that we should present an advertisement where we vividly show the audience all the different creative uses of a hoola-hoop. I then assigned Cindy to be the artist to come up with a poster to act as a template for the advertisement that displayed all the great and fun things that can be done with the hoola-hoop (she owns a creative soap-making company so I figured she would be best suited for design). I then assigned Rhonda (who had been working in the corporate world for many years and was well versed on the topic of "pitching ideas to management") to be the spokesperson for our project team. She needed to figure out a way to sell the idea to our boss. Becky was then assigned to develop the slogan for the new product as well as how to pitch the product to our targeted audience. She was a fitness fanatic who loved social gatherings and was planning to raise a family soon. She was our targeted customer! I then assigned myself to write a formal proposal to send to the owners. I have had some writing experience!

This division of labor took about three minutes. Then the team had twelve minutes to finish their assignments. We were all done within eight minutes. It seemed so much easier when we had a very definite plan and we knew exactly what we had to do. We had a system and we followed that system. There was no time to think about whether or not the system was right. We knew that in order for us to be successful in the time allotted that we needed to stick to the plan at all costs. The time for determining whether or not the system worked was obviously after the project had been completed, when there was some date available to analyze. Only afterwards would we know whether or not the system worked. And if it didn't, we knew that it would be quite easy to analyze exactly why it didn't work. We would have a full sample of data available to help us determine which parts of the system needed tweaking. So we went with it. We stuck to the plan. And you know what? We felt great about our results! We felt organized and we felt prepared. Before, we felt chaotic. Sure, we felt energized before but we were horribly unfocused. Now we felt efficient.

When Maria came back the second time she smiled at us and asked if we had learned anything. We all felt like second-graders ("Yes, Ms. Maria") but the truth was that we did learn something. We learned something about organization. We learned something about sticking to a plan.

Maria didn't even want to hear our new proposals. She wanted us to simply analyze the system that we had used, understand how that system positively affected our results, and make sure that we knew exactly what needed to be done the next time. She wanted us to have a plan.

Do you see what we did? Instead of having 25 different proposed solutions or ideas, we had one very solid plan that we would be ready to implement. We had something solid! Would you feel good about going to your boss and saying, "I have 25 great ideas on how to solve our marketing woes but have no idea what to do about them"?

No way would you feel good about that! And I can pretty much guarantee that your boss wouldn't feel good about that either. She'd probably say something like "Give me something I can use" and "Come back to talk to me when you have a plan that I can actually implement instead of ideas to just think about". Have a plan; what a concept!

My head was obviously spinning again on my way home from class that night. I knew I needed to sit down in my thinking chair. The lessons I learned would surely have an impact on my investment strategy, or so I figured.

When I got home and sat down in my chair I immediately remembered the words that resonated through my head all night: Have a plan!

Without a doubt, no trader will last long if he doesn't plan every trade. It is a lot like Covey's (pg. 139) mission statement. Covey (pg. 139) says that "mission statements are vital to the success of organizations". That isn't only true in business. *Any* organization (even just the organization of your trading system) could benefit from a mission statement. Make your trading plan your personal trading mission statement. In other words, when you go to develop your trading plan, first develop a goal or a mission statement so that you know why you are trading in the first place. The plan will be that much easier to create when you have clear and concise goals in mind.

But the goal is only as important as you take it. One of the things I learned in the class was that if you are not disciplined enough to follow the plan that you have created then there is no reason to have a plan in the first place. It would just be a waste of time! But it is about so much more than just discipline. It is also about commitment. If you are committed to sticking to the plan from the very beginning then you will have no real reason to stray. You need to not give yourself that option to get away from the plan. Just take comfort in knowing that the plan you have chosen is the one you will use no matter what happens with a particular investment. You also know that only after all the data is in can you really evaluate the performance of the plan itself. Take it as a learning experience. You wouldn't be upset if you went to school and were taught something that goes against what you originally thought, would you? Of course not! You go to school so that you *can* learn new things. You sit through class patiently being told things that you didn't know before. Afterwards (perhaps in your thinking chair!) you can take a look at what you have learned and determine how you are going to make use of that information. So look at investing as your school. Create a plan, follow it, and patiently sit through as the plan unfolds. Afterwards, you know that you can always make adjustments. More times than not, though, the reason the plan failed is because you didn't follow it to a tee.

I know that you must be dying to start trading but be patient! If this book were your life as a trader, you would be in the theory phase of your development as a successful trader. Once you complete the theories of successful trading (section I of this book) then you can begin to develop your system to use with actual trades (section II). So don't worry. It will come!

The plan, however, can't just be any old plan that you choose out of a hat. The plan you create should cater for every eventuality. There should be no surprises. If you create a plan and watch as the plan unfolds only to be surprised by some of the things that happen to your portfolio then you need to rewrite your plan. As Richard Dennis (of Turtles' fame) once said, "Don't worry about where the prices are going. Worry about what you are going to do when they get there". In other words, include every scenario in your plan. Surprises are fun in the entertainment world but trust me, they aren't always so much fun in the world of investing. Remember, this book is how to become a *stressfree* trader. Surprises, by definition, create stress.

Think a moment about what is being said on these pages. When you decide to put your money down on an investment, do you have any control over the prices or the markets? For the vast majority of you, the answer will be a resounding "no". So stop worrying about what could happen that is truly beyond your control and concentrate on your trigger points and what you will do when these points are violated. By doing this your trading stops being emotional and starts to become very systematic and mechanical. Now I'm not suggesting that you remove all emotions from the entire investment process. You are certainly going to feel the urge to do cartwheels and jump up and down when you discover that your plan worked and you've earned 100% on your investments within one year. You don't have to hold those urges inside in order for this process to work. So go ahead and sing and dance and do cartwheels when things go your way!

I'm simply suggesting that you develop a plan and don't let your fears and other emotions get in the way of seeing that plan out. Emotion is great, just don't let it cloud your judgment and force you to alter your plan half way through. Stick to your plan and you will be well on your way to stressfree trading.

Let's look at a trading scenario that you may come across. Included are some of the questions you need to ask yourself in order to properly design your trading plan. Once you have your plan, answering these questions will be a snap[1]:

1. You like the look of stock YIC, Inc., which is currently trading at $40

2. You place a buy 100, stop in at $42 (meaning you will be willing to pay as much as $42 per share)…but this is just the beginning. At this point you must ask yourself the following questions (you also have to answer them!):

    a. IF filled on this trade then where will I place my initial stop loss (i.e. when do I get out or how much of my capital am I willing to lose?)

---

1. Once again, if you are struggling to develop a plan of your own, please don't worry because we have not gotten there yet! This section is all about hypotheticals, systems, plans, theory, and organization. Section II of this book is where you will find actual trading systems and strategies that you can use once you have learned the underlying principles of stressfree trading.

b.   IF filled on this trade then how will I take profits? By how much will I trail my stop? What exit strategies will I use?

c.   IF filled, will I add more shares as the trade goes my way?

d.   IF filled and the share does not show a profit after X weeks, will I get out, or will I let my trailing stop exit me from the trade?

e.   IF stopped out of this trade will I be willing to try and get back in, or completely scratch the trade and look elsewhere?[2]

3.   So let's say you have created your plan by answering these questions (and others) and prior to entering the trade you place the order to buy 100 YIC, Inc. at $42

4.   Let's also say that you are filled at $42 1/4, automatically you place a stop order in at $39 (meaning that once the stock drops down to $39 you will automatically sell). As long as you stick to your plan there should be no guessing. This step will be automatic

5.   The trade goes your way and a second buy order is placed in at $50 (again, automatic according to your plan)

6.   You buy 100 more YIC, Inc. at $50 and the stop is now moved up to $45 (you will now automatically sell your shares if the price drops down to $45).

7.   The trade goes your way and you keep raising your stop at a safe distance behind each time

8.   The stock continues to rise to $80 so you place your stop at $74 (no guessing, it will all be a part of your plan)

---

2.   If none of these questions make sense to you, don't worry. They all involve investment terms and ideas that you will learn when you go to develop your trading system.

9. Your sell stop is hit at $74 and you exit the trade with a massive profit (again all part of your plan because your plan should tell you exactly where you will exit)

The point of this example is to obviously show you that once a plan is created, everything becomes easier. There are no questions of "should I do this" or "look what's happening, I don't know if this will work". It all comes down to automatic responses to data. If this, then this. If A, then B. You'll know exactly where to get in, where to place the stops, where and when to add, and how to exit. You will now be conclusively trading like a professional and not from emotion. This is one of the reasons why you never hear a professional trader complain about the market. Remember, a faulty craftsman blames his tools…

If the previous example seemed too complicated or too simplified for you (depending upon your trading experience) don't fret. It was merely an exercise meant to explain that you need to stop guessing in order to become a stressfree trader. Imagine if you had to guess what to do at each point in the example above. It would be terrible. I don't know about you but I hate not knowing what is going on or what to do in a situation. That's scary. Of course, if you love to fly by the seat of your pants, you hate to have things organized, you want luck to run your world, and you want nature to run its course then you may want to consider Vegas instead of Wall Street!

And not once did you have to ask for an opinion. Not one time did you have to turn to the newspaper to read about all the advice that investment planners are giving the general public. Not once were you afraid of letting a profit get away, or of a loss becoming too big. Simply put, if you make a plan and have the discipline and commitment to follow it then trading becomes very *easy*…and ultimately stressfree.

One thing that I have always come across throughout my years of trading is that the market will go to great lengths to throw you off track. You will hear all sorts of contradicting advice. You will read all sorts of reports about what the markets are going to do. Others will constantly be trying to convince you to trade their way. Once you are in a share, it is kind of like riding a wild horse. The horse will thrash around violently. All the scared and emotional riders will be instantly bucked to the ground. They will have to pick themselves up and start over. Or they will be so confused as to what happened that they won't know what to do next.

Trading is no different (except for the smell!). The emotional and scared traders will instantly be bucked off the markets. They will violently fall down and try to dust themselves off so that they can start over. They may decide to go with a different horse or even try a different career altogether. It will only be the ones who have the discipline and the commitment to follow a set plan that will benefit from the full move. Only those committed riders will reap the rewards (plus with trading you will likely get more out of it than cheers from a crowd or a free beer).

As I said before, you should never have to ask someone's opinion about a trade. If you do find that you have to ask for someone's opinion, then you have either not created a plan that works or you don't have the commitment or confidence in your plan to ride it out. And if you find that your second guessing of the plan leads to changes in your actions then you would have been better off having never made the trade in the first place. It is not worth the stress and it will probably fail anyway. Commit yourself or keep searching!

Think about planning a trade like planning a vacation. What happens if you lose your credit cards? What happens if, once you get to the Bahamas, you remember that you left the stove on? What happens if your luggage gets lost? What happens if you win a lot of money at the casino? What do you do with your dog? What do you do about the mail?

It's kind of like that with trading. Make a plan and take all the guesswork (and stress) out of the equation. What happens if the share gaps down? What about flys up? What happens if the market crashes? What happens if the company announces an accounting error? What happens if the company announces a merger that forces the price to go up by $20 in one day? If you are not prepared for these situations then you will be caught by surprise and you will be left wondering what to do. And you may not want to find out what kind of decisions you make under pressure. You also won't want to miss the boat. After all, just like with vacation planning, if you start trading from the hip and not from the plan then you can expect your results to worsen. If you left the stove on but you gave your neighbor a checklist of the things to check up on (cat, mail, newspaper, stove, water, etc.) then you will have nothing to worry about. The plan will take care of all surprises. And you don't have to spend countless time and energy trying to figure out what to do next. You will know exactly what to do if you leave your purse on the beaches of Puerta Vallerta! You'll have that much less stress.

Remember, having a plan completely removes all the emotion and opinion from the trade. This is a good thing! Time and time again I hear things like, "I bought ABC stock at $25 a few months ago, do you think I should still keep it?"

I really feel for these traders. If they are asking this question then they obviously do not have a plan. It seems so logical. When this person got into the trade, didn't he have any plan for when and how he was going to get out? What does he think is going to happen and when it does (or doesn't) then will he be prepared? Not at all! This trader is not trading. This trader is gambling. He has bought a lottery ticket and doesn't even know when he is going to decide to check the papers to see if he has won or not. Obviously, if this trader had a plan and the discipline to follow it then he never would have had to ask this question. He would have more likely said, "I bought ABC stock at $25 a few months ago, added to it a couple weeks later, and sold it for $34 yesterday" or he would have said, "I bought ABC stock a few months ago and had to sell because it hit my exit number after one week". Either outcome could be considered a successful one because he had a plan and stuck to it. The first outcome would have been great because he would now have more money than he started with. The second would have been great because he now would have more knowledge than he started with, and he likely would have traded a few more times since then and come out way ahead. If he has to ask what to do *after* he has already purchased the stock, few outcomes would be positive.

It seems silly but I truly believe that people like being told what to do. Wait a minute! Strike that. Maybe it is not so dramatic. Maybe people don't always like being told what to do but they just like being social and like discussing things like stocks and trading. If that is your motivation then that is what suits you. But you are not really trading. If you are using stocks to spark conversation, then those stocks could be considered party favors. And there is nothing wrong with that if that is what you have decided! But if you trade stocks to invest and to make money then you need to make a plan for yourself and stop listening to others' trading advice.

While reading a recent Internet magazine I was astounded to discover the number of followers some of the tip sheets had. The top ones have from 15,000 to 80,000! Are any of those followers really making themselves better traders? Will they ever improve their trading techniques? Will they ever improve their results? Some will succeed and some will fail, but to leave your fate in the hands of someone who claims to be an expert is just plain odd. There is no analysis. You don't have any assurance that the person you are following cares at all about you or your success. You have no idea why you fail with some trades and why you succeed with others. Don't you want to know?! Don't you want to have at least some control over your trades and your future? Now some may argue that they believe they could never be as good at trading as the experts so why not just follow those experts? Why not just ride on their coattails? But how do you think those experts became experts? By following tip sheets? By listening to the advice of others? No way! They became experts because they developed their plan and stuck to it no matter what. They had a system and they made it work for themselves. They had a plan. They took responsibility for themselves. Now you can do the same thing! You can become the expert! Even if you don't think you could ever be as good as the top millionaire traders, at the very least you can have control of your own future.

When you start following your own plan you will start to find yourself tuning out the advice of others. If you hold ADF stock and bought at $60 and your initial stop loss is at $56 then why would you care if the local trading guru tells you to sell ADF because it is overvalued and will fall to $20? For one thing those gurus are just as likely to be right as they are to be wrong (just look at all the newspaper picks…they are usually right around the market average). If your stop was at $56 then let this kick you out of the trade. Don't let the advice of someone make you alter your plan. Stick to your plan because you will set your own rules for success. At the very least you can then answer yes to the question that you will ask yourself every day: Did I follow my rules today?

I can guarantee you that before Warren Buffet, or George Soros buys $50,000,000 worth of stocks they know exactly what they will do if prices swing one way or another. Could you imagine Warren Buffet thinking, "gee, I bought $20,000,000 worth of DFG stock and it's down by 15%. What shall I do?" Not a chance! He has a plan and will stick to it. If his plan was to exit at a loss of no more than 1% than he sure as heck won't be asking anybody when he should be getting out of DFG. So why should it be any different with your trading? Don't think in dollars. Think in sense! Whether you are trading with $50,000,000 or $5,000 the principles will still apply. The percentages will be the same. A loss of $1,000 on your trade is the same as a loss on $10,000,000 for Mr. Buffet's trade (and will hurt you both about the same)! The plan is what matters. You must work hard to eliminate all emotion and follow *your* plan.

To be a winner in the markets you can never trade from emotion. And the only way to truly eliminate emotion is to have a plan and have the determination and discipline to follow that plan. It's rather unfortunate that many traders do not have a plan. But what's even more unfortunate is when you find a trader who has a solid plan but then lets emotion get in the way. They were so close!

If you want to be one of the market winners then you must plan every trade and trade every plan!

5

Work Hard at Learning How to Trade...and Keep Working!

How do you learn more about a topic that you think you have some knowledge about already? This was what was written up on the chalkboard when we entered class the next week. Most of us immediately began to think and talk about possible answers. How do we become better at something? What do we have to do to continue learning? Read books? Talk to others in the field? Attend seminars? Join group discussions?

Maria was predicting these answers because the first thing she said to us was, "What do all those answers have in common?"

Before any of us were able to answer that question, Maria told us to pull out a piece of paper. She then instructed us to make little holes for our eyes. It seemed strange (but most of her little games seemed rather strange at first so we always just played along) but we knew it was going to lead to something so we did what she asked. Then she instructed us to count off in eights (1,2,3,4,5,6,7,8,1,2,3...) because there were sixteen people in the class. After that we were to get together with the other person that shared our same number. We were given a very specific topic of conversation. We were to talk about something that we had done that we wish we would have done differently. Some project that we feel as though we didn't do so well. Some meeting where we felt we should have prepared more. We just had to pick a situation where we messed up! However, the catch was that we had to place the paper mask in front of our faces. We then had to converse for twenty minutes (five to tell the story, five to discuss the response from the other person, five to hear the other person's story, and five to discuss our response) all the while holding that piece of paper in front of our faces so that the other person could see nothing but our eyes.

Next time you go to work you should grab your boss and the other higher ups to play this game with you. I'm sure they won't mind![1] Anyway, we were absolutely amazed at what we heard. I told the story of how I once conducted a meeting at my former employment and really felt as though I failed. I had decided to have three facilitators (one representative from human resources, one from accounting, and one from operations) to help lead the meeting in the directions I wanted to go and cover the topics I wanted to cover. It was chaos!

But after I told the story, I really started to hear what suggestions the other person had. Some were things that I had already thought of and some were things that had never crossed my mind. I was able to fully listen to that person because my eyes were not distracted at all. I was not confused by what that person was saying. I did not get caught up in facial expressions or eye contact or pieces of food in that person's teeth. I simply listened to the words. Of course, the conversation had a lot of "what do you mean" and "could you explain" so it was not exactly the fastest conversation in the world. But it was certainly not a confusing one. I clearly understood what the other person was saying and she clearly understood what I was saying. I was able to take her suggestions to heart and really apply them to situations in my daily living. I was able to utilize what I had learned in order to work towards

---

1.   Neither the authors or anyone associated with or referenced by this book can be held responsible for your boss's reaction or for your impending dismissal!

improving my skills and abilities. There was nothing to confuse the issue. There was no thinking "I wonder what she meant by that". It was all in the words. And those words gave me the tools necessary to work towards improvement.

Of course, Maria had to ruin it all by telling us that it was a principle that she wanted us to learn. Rats! I was hoping that I had discovered something revolutionary. She explained that some of it had to do with eliminating outside noise and some of it had to do with proper communication and understanding how to apply and manage feedback. What is so funny in our regular conversations during our daily lives is that many of the statements we make to others is rather vague. Ambiguous statements are extremely common in everyday conversation, which is unfortunate because they lead to horrible misunderstandings (Devito, 2002, pg. 53). How often have you told someone that you would be there soon? How often have you heard that something won't cost a lot of money? But what does "soon" really mean? What do you think when you hear "won't cost much"? Well, for one thing I can pretty much guarantee that these terms will mean something slightly (or extremely!) different for your then they do for the person you are speaking with. These are extremely vague terms and need to be cleared up if communication will ever survive!

The masks made these vague statements really stand out. We couldn't help but ask the other person to clear things up and let us know exactly what they mean. There was nothing to interfere. We just had the words and, lacking any other stimuli, we wanted to make sure that we got the words right. We were properly and effectively managing our feedback (Devito, pgs. 54–55)! We were working towards improvement. We were making sure there were no ambiguities, no misunderstandings. Once we had clear and concise feedback, we were then able to focus on how that feedback could improve our actions.

But it didn't stop there. Once we realized that feedback could really help us if properly managed, we kept working towards getting information that could help us. We were on a roll! And it wasn't just the feedback that we were receiving from the other people. Once I learned how to manage feedback, I was able to understand and apply my *own* feedback that much better. I was able to learn better. And one thing I learned from the feedback (from the other person as well as myself) was that I needed to continue to work towards success. I needed to get past all the interference in my head (like bills, what I'm doing next weekend, if the Cubs will ever win, etc.) and really focus on trying to improve my skills and abilities. I needed to really listen to my own feedback.

I didn't wait until I got to my thinking chair that night. My thinking chair became my car seat. I knew right away that working hard towards improvement and really understanding feedback (both from others and from myself) would pave the path towards trading success. I knew that I had to work hard at improvement and continue to work throughout my trading career. After all, it is no different in any other profession. I certainly wouldn't expect a doctor to think that she has learned everything there is to know about medicine just because she went to medical school. I would expect her to continue to learn and work hard at improving her skills. I would expect her to manage her feedback and use the information that she gains along the way to improve her skills and abilities. I would absolutely feel more comfortable as a patient of this doctor who constantly strives for improvement all throughout her medical career as opposed to someone who refuses to learn anything more once he graduates from medical school. Imagine going in to see a doctor about a migraine and the doctor telling you that he learned in medical school thirty years ago that the best way to alleviate migraine pain is to drill small holes in your head! You'd run like mad out of there that instant!

Likewise, would you expect someone to become a brain surgeon after he attends a few seminars and reads a few books?! Of course not! Just like any profession (whether you do it for a career or on the side), trading requires constant work and constant improvement. Trading also requires practice and education. Why do so many people think that they can become a market wizard just because they read a book or went to one seminar? Continuous learning is vital towards maintained success in the stock market.

But, as I learned in my class, trading also requires good feedback management; feedback from educational sources like successful traders, seminars, and books. But most importantly, successful trading requires effective management of feedback from within yourself. As I said before, you need to develop a plan and stick to it. But you also have to take the time to analyze your plan and work towards improving it. You may lose money at first. You may feel unsuccessful at first. You may feel that you have a lot to learn. Most successful traders will tell you that it took quite a long time, determination, effort, and failure before they were able to become as successful as they are. It really is not much different than becoming a successful lawyer, doctor, or businessman. I don't know very many successful lawyers who just graduated from law school! It takes time and work. I know what you must be thinking, "Last chapter he told us to ignore the advice of others". You are exactly right, but let me explain.

Everybody needs the help of others at some point in their lives. But you just have to be selective as to who you are listening to. For instance, if you wanted to study the causes of migraine headaches, you probably would want to get the information from leading professionals or professional publications like the American Medical Association journals. You certainly aren't going to want to get the information from the National Enquirer or a daytime soap opera! So just be selective in your learning process. You have the choice. You can learn from the best or you can learn from the guy who sent you an email yesterday claiming to make you a millionaire in two days if you just send him a $50 check! Sure, you have to put the work in and learn how to be a successful trader but you just want to make sure that you are not wasting your time, money, or opportunities.

But before you can put the work into your profession you must first decide that you really do want to be a trader (and again, I don't necessarily mean as your only career or as a career at all. I mean, I consider myself a basketball player but it is certainly not one of my *careers*!). One thing you may want to ask yourself is whether or not you are really interested in trading. Is it something that you are genuinely attracted to or are you just lured into the game because of the big pay-offs? The reason I ask is because it has been my experience that those people who truly enjoy something seem to have more success and better results. There are lots of ways to make money in this world. You might as well choose something that you love to do.

I remember reading the book from Napolean Hill titled *Grow Rich with Peace of Mind* (1996). The author had interviewed the top people in a number of different professions and came to the conclusion that those people who are at the top of their fields really seem to love their jobs. They would have done the work for no money. They chose something that they really enjoyed doing so that their everyday lives were happy. They were able to poor their hearts and souls into their profession. That is why they were so successful! Do you think someone who hates their job could ever be successful?

I'm sure you have come across people who have hated their jobs and they appear to be successful. Perhaps they make a lot of money. Perhaps they are well respected in their fields. But just imagine how much more successful they could be if they truly loved what they were doing. Success is a very difficult thing to measure but I suppose success could somehow be measured against one's potential. If someone hates their job, sure they may make a lot of money but what they are making is but a fraction of what they *could* be making…if only they chose something that they enjoyed doing.

Trading can be looked at in the same way. If your number one goal is to make as much money as possible in the markets then I doubt you will ever reach your potential. You'll just be punching your timeclock. It won't mean anything more to you than money. Now that's not to say that money shouldn't be one of your goals. Or that money is bad or money is a bad motivator. Clearly money is on just about everybody's minds.

But if you don't also like what you are doing then you may not be fulfilling your potential. You may reach your goal of making money but why not have more than one goal? Life is so short that it only makes sense to have multiple goals attached to something that you will spend any amount of time doing. Go ahead and make money, but love to trade so that you are motivated to learn and work on what really produces. If your only motivation is money then you may be missing out on a great deal. You may be tempted to keep chasing the latest hot new trading idea that exploits the fact that some people are only motivated by money. Don't let them trick you! If you are motivated to become a great trader through hard work, time, effort, and determination then you won't be lured in by these scams.

I am absolutely amazed by the number of traders who have not even educated themselves on the very basics of the stock market. For some reason it takes too much time or too much effort for these people to open a book and learn something. Or perhaps they just love the thrill of buying into the latest fad. If that is in fact the case then they really are not traders at all; they are gamblers. I always find it quite humorous to find people who are so willing to shell out $10,000 on an investment that some stranger told them about but they are not willing to pick up a book or take a class to learn a little bit about what they are throwing their money into.

Again, there are plenty of people out there who have legitimate reasons for doing this (like gamblers and those who do it more for the sport or because they can). But the sad cases are the ones who lose that $10,000 within six months because they were chasing a pipe dream. Just like anything else, a successful trader is an educated trader.

The very best traders went through years and years of trial and error until they became consistently successful traders. They lost some money here and there. They gained some money here and there. They learned all the while. So why should it be any different for you?

Learn to keep learning!

6
Think Positive

When I walked into the next class session, there were a few words written on the blackboard that had us all thinking: You've Heard It Before. While we were all pretty used to wondering what was going to unfold during the class session, I was amazed to find so many people openly trying to figure out what exactly it was that we had all heard before. Something about education maybe. Possibly something about persistence. Perhaps it was something about organization or timeliness or any number of things we have heard since we were six years old and off to school for the first time. But then Maria came in and asked six people to join her in the front of the room.

She then began to explain a problem that she was having. She was in the process of writing her dissertation for a PhD program and was having difficulties with her professors. They wanted her to change her entire format, but they were unwilling to explain to her exactly what it was they were looking for. They did, however, explain that she probably would not be able to graduate at the time she originally was told she was going to. She didn't know what to do. She had put so much time and effort into completing her assignments that she was a little taken aback when she was faced with the possibility that she may have to start all over again. Eight months of hard work for nothing!

She then asked the people who she had brought to the front of the class what they thought of the situation. You wouldn't believe the amount of (mostly good) advice that she received! It was amazing. Those students came up with all sorts of ideas on how to fix the problem, how to talk to her professors, how to ask for more time, how to convince them that her project was a worthy one. Everybody heard some wonderful ideas and almost everybody in the class chimed in with their thoughts as well. Everybody seemed to agree that the problem needed to be solved.

After Maria thanked all of us for our helpful suggestions, she asked the people up front to take their seats. She then began to tell us the optometrist story from Covey's *The Seven Habits of Highly Effective People* (1989, pgs. 236–237). It went something like this:

> Let's say you had something wrong with your eyes. They hurt all the time like you constantly had something in them and you could barely see far enough to read your morning newspaper. So you decide to go see an optometrist to get some help (certainly a reasonable solution). When you get to the optometrist, you explain the problem to her. She looks at you and smiles. She then takes off her glasses and gives them to you. "Put these on…they have helped me be able to see for nearly ten years". So you put the glasses on and your eyes become even worse. You now feel like you are seeing through the bottom of a Pepsi bottle. You explain that the glasses aren't helping any and the optometrist says, "Maybe you just aren't trying hard enough. Try harder. Think positive!" After explaining that the glasses just aren't going to work for you the optometrist says, "You just don't know how to think positive. You are too negative. No wonder things don't work out for you". She then takes her glasses back and storms out of the examination room. (Covey, 1989, pgs. 236–237)

After she tells the story, Maria takes off her glasses (funny) and asks what happened in the story, all the while pointing to the words on the blackboard: You've Heard It Before. After a few blank stares fell her way, Maria explained that the problem with the optometrist was that she decided to prescribe before she diagnosed (Covey, 1989, pgs. 236–237). She did not take any time to try and figure out the problem. Instead, she headed straight towards a solution. Unfortunately, it was a solution for a different problem!

Maria then went on to explain that those infamous words that all of us have heard a million times before, Think Positive, don't really mean much unless we truly understand what is going on inside of us. And we have to be realistic! It wouldn't do anybody any good to think positive all the while they are robbing banks. Thinking positive is a wonderful solution…as long as it is appropriate for the problem.

This seemed so simple, but how many times have you told someone to think positive before you truly understand the problem that they are telling you? I must have said those words to my wife thirty thousand times before I realized that thinking positive wasn't exactly the appropriate solution to her problem. When she would come home from a long day of work and complain about her schedule and her clients and having to go through the same headache again the next day I would usually think to myself "Why can't she just be positive?"

Of course, being positive wouldn't have solved the problem! The systems have to be in place. The organization has to be settled. The ground rules have to be laid. Only then will thinking positive help! I can't expect to do everything wrong, think positive, and presto! Everything works! Positive self belief is built from repetition after repetition of following the rules and doing things right. This is exactly how it has to be when trading!

Iron clad positive belief in your system will work just so long as you have built your system to succeed. You must develop the rules and then believe in them without exception. Hard discipline to execute both entry and exits flawlessly according to your system are essential to your trading success. And without positive self belief, you will not be able to execute these decisions. But positive self belief isn't going to help if you are doing everything the wrong way (like constantly buying into the latest trading fad)! You need to develop a sound system and then believe in it. Create something solid and then be proud of it...and believe in it to the end.

The top traders know that it is the discipline displayed in following their rules that is the important thing in trading and the money rewards are secondary. They also know that they need to believe in their systems in order to have the discipline to follow them. Imagine being a vacuum salesman. If you know darn well that the vacuums that are being sold at the store down the street are much better and cheaper than your vacuums, I guarantee you will have a much more difficult time selling your vacuums. The customers will know that you aren't convinced that your vacuums are the best. And if you aren't convinced, then they won't be convinced[1].

Let me say it one more time: Positive self belief is built from repetition after repetition of following your rules. Extensive back-testing of your system and constant self analyses is vital.

You will never be able to follow your system if you have even a shred of doubt in your mind. That's why so many people who buy other people's systems fail. When that system goes through a losing period the person who purchased it will begin to lose faith in it. They won't

---

1.   Of course, there is the rare individual that can sell something that (s)he does not believe in. But those people won't be reading this book...they'll be out selling fake get-rich-quick schemes for hundreds of dollars!

believe that the system actually works. They will likely throw the system in the garbage and begin searching for a new system. But the problem is that we "have such a tendency to rush in, to fix things up" (Covey, 1989, pg. 237) without truly discovering the underlying problem. It wouldn't do any good to think positively about someone else's problem! The great traders will have their systems. They'll believe in them. And they won't "rush in" and "fix things up" (Covey, 1989, pg. 237) whenever things seem to be going bad. They'll understand the roots of the problems. They'll understand that if they believe in their system then they will likely just need to exhibit a little patience. But most of all, they won't just dump the system in search of another one.

The trader who has developed his own system and believes in it with all his trading heart will know darn well that the system may go through losing periods. He has seen it all before and will sit it out, waiting for the conditions to become more favorable. He will not panic. And most of all, he will still believe in his system. This is where positive self belief *is* the correct solution to the problem! The system is there. It is set. Now the trader must just believe in it to work and reap the rewards once it does. The person who has dumped the one system and bought another has likely dumped that one as well because it, too, has gone through a losing period. That person has now wasted money purchasing two systems that someone else has developed and is now in search of a third. All he had to do was develop the system so that it worked for him and then truly believe in whatever system he had chosen to use. Then he could have waited through the losing periods and gotten right back in to make money when things got better. But he didn't believe. He will be forever searching.

A big part of positive self belief is confidence. How do you get confident? If you are like me, it is through practice and hard work. You must strive to work through as much market data as is possible with your system so you know exactly what is normal and what is not. You will need to recognize changes. You will need to practice. A couple of years ago I started playing basketball again at a local gym. It had been several years since I had last played but I knew that I used to be pretty good. After that first game though, my confidence was shot. I couldn't shoot anymore. I couldn't dribble anymore. My passes were flying out of bounds. I felt like my feet were stuck in cement. I had totally lost my game.

But it wasn't because I was no longer a good basketball player (although that is likely what most people at the gym were thinking). No, it was because I hadn't practiced. I needed to practice more and more to build up my confidence so that I could once again become successful. Practice creates confidence. You get to see your success right in front of your eyes. You start to recognize when things are going your way and when things are not. You become sharp. And when that happens, you become successful.

This is why the greatest traders alive seem to go through large losing streaks while never batting an eyelid. They have practiced. They are so confident that they know exactly what they are doing, even when the results are not one hundred percent perfect. Do you think Michael Jordan lost confidence in his ability every time he missed a free throw? Of course not! Now most people would agree that George Soros is the greatest trader alive. Think of him as the Michael Jordan of trading. Mr. Soros made billions in the 1980's and 1990's, yet he has also had some mind boggling losing periods! His fund at times has also lost billions of dollars and posted big negative returns! But did it bother him?

Well, now that I think of it I'm sure he didn't exactly *enjoy* losing billions of dollars but one thing is for sure: He never panicked. He knew that his style of trading will go through losing periods. Just as dawn follows dusk, a losing period is usually followed by a winning one and vice-versa. Yet too many traders tend to throw in the towel after taking a couple of successive losers. They never seem to be around when the system kicks back into a winning period.

I guess it goes back to another adage that you have likely heard a million times before: What you see is what you get. If you look at your problem areas you will see that they are rooted in faulty and/or limited beliefs. If you are having problems with your trading results perhaps it is time to examine your beliefs about your trading system and about trading in general. If you lack that complete confidence in your system that is vital towards your trading success then you need to stop trading and figure out why you do not have that confidence. Why don't you believe? Maybe you have negative feelings about trading in general. Maybe you really do believe that it is all a big crap shoot and you have just as much chance to win or lose as anyone else. If this is the case, trading is not for you.

A person who is a compulsive gambler will never make it trading in the markets. These types of traders seem to think that nothing is their fault. If they lose a huge amount of capital then they will try to find blame. However, if they truly looked inside themselves to try and determine what their true feelings are, they would probably realize that they view trading as a big casino. These are negative beliefs! These beliefs will not allow you to succeed. If you think that your success is based upon luck then you are in the wrong game!

"Everyone gets what they want in life"

—Ed Seykota[2]

You will likely find that most people will get what they want out of trading. You just have to examine what it is that you truly want, and then you have to believe enough to get that. You have to ask yourself

---

2.   Mr. Seykota is well known in investment circles as being a rather successful professional trader.

what your beliefs are about trading. Are you being constantly told that trading is a no-win game? Are you told that trend following doesn't work? Are you told that you can't win? Does it matter what you are told?

Take a moment now to write down your beliefs about trading. I'll help you get started (although you may not want to write in this book because that will lower its Ebay value!):

1. What kind of returns are possible?

2. How much time do I have to invest in developing my system and working with it?

3. How much time and effort do I think I need to put in to receive a day's pay?

Let me stop you right there. When I first started trading, I phoned my broker constantly. I checked the quotes every ten or fifteen minutes. I read every report that came out. I had the business channel running in the background 24-7. I felt I needed to work hour after hour every single day in order to make it work. I thought I needed to put in a lot of hard work in order to receive pay. It took a long time to shake that belief out!

If you believe it's relatively simple to make 50% p.a. from the stock market year in and year out, with very low risk and with just ten minutes of work per day then that is great; because it is possible and you will likely succeed. But if you believe that you need to check the reports every five minutes and talk to your broker every fifteen minutes then you will likely do that and you will think that you are really staying on top of it all. But you will also likely be miserable because of all that work you are doing. It is all about belief systems. You get what you want!

On the other hand, if you believe that working only ten minutes for a comfortable wage is a lazy way to make a living and you feel uncomfortable even thinking about it then you will obviously have to resolve this conflict if you are ever going to obtain these results.

Choose your beliefs wisely. In all problems with your trading you are both the problem and the solution. The top traders know this. If they go through an extensive period of losers they'll start analyzing their beliefs. They will start to look inside for the answers. Do they really believe? Is there something fundamentally wrong with their belief systems? They'll begin to fix the problem from the inside out.

Now, the real question is how do you begin to develop a positive self-belief?

Well, for one thing it takes a lot of work. You will have to start taking responsibility (refer to previous chapter) for your trading and then you will have to develop and test a trading system. The rest is built from practice and experience. You will believe in yourself once you are confident. You will be confident once you are comfortable. You will be comfortable once you have experience. And you can't get experience without practice!

Just for a brief moment, think of trading as a basketball game. Don't think of it as a get-rich-quick scheme. This entire process takes time. Pretend you are playing basketball. In order to gain confidence, you have to practice. In order for you to practice, you have to put those shorts on and get yourself to the gym! You can't practice basketball by watching the Bulls or Lakers play. You have to get in the game.

It's the same with trading. You have to get in the game. Start out by using your system on small trades that hardly seem worth your while. You will gain an awful lot more than money with these trades because you will gain confidence. You will gain a positive self belief…and once you develop your winning system, your unwavering positive belief in yourself and your system will reap the rewards you are looking for.

7

It's Nothing Personal!

The next class session found most of the students staring at the black-board as they entered the room. There were just five words written on the board but they were words that (unfortunately) most of us had heard at one point in our lives. Those five words have sparked several movie, television, and book ideas throughout history. Just five words. Five words that could have a thousand different meanings. Five words that demand "thinking into" and "reading between the lines". Face value is never really a possibility with those five words.

So when we sat in our chairs and read *It's Not You, It's Me* over and over again; we couldn't help but try and figure out what the meaning was behind those words (as most people would upon encountering them).

What does that phrase really mean? Does the speaker of those words really believe that (s)he is to blame? Or, as most people would suspect, are those words simply used to soften the blow? On the other hand, perhaps that phrase has become such a cliche over the years that people now really do believe that they are the problem when uttering those words. Maybe they are sincere. Or maybe they just want you to think that so that the blow is softened! This is the torment that most people go through when they hear those words.

This was the torment that George Costanza went through when he said, "Don't give me the it's-not-you-it's-me routine…if it's anybody, it's me"! Similarly, this was the torment that the students in my class went through that evening when seeing those words on the blackboard.

As usual, though, Maria walked into the classroom right about the time we began to get antsy. She immediately handed out a worksheet to each of the sixteen students in the class. The worksheet contained a picture of a man wearing a business suit walking rather briskly through the park while looking at his watch. There was a space at the bottom of the picture just above the instructions: Describe what this man is doing.

It sounded simple enough. Maria gave us five minutes to write down our answers. So I began to explain that the man was probably on his way to work and was perhaps running a little late. It took me thirty seconds to write that down so I spent the next four and a half minutes thinking about how the Cubs really seemed to be heading in the right direction for the 2003 season (after all, they had recently signed some pretty good players to add to their already impressive roster). I'm a Cub fan. I'm a dreamer. I'm a glutton for punishment. It goes with the territory.

After the five minutes were up, Maria divided us into two groups of eight students each. We were then instructed to assign a speaker for our group who would be in charge of describing the picture to the class. Maria also explained to us that she wanted us to try and convince her that our group had the most accurate description of the picture. After each group was finished describing the picture then all members of both groups would be allowed to share their thoughts. We were told to only describe the "action" of the picture. In other words, we were only allowed to talk about what we thought the person in the picture was doing, where he had been, where he was going, and so on.

The discussion began innocently enough. We gave our description of the picture and then the other group gave their explanation. The funny thing was, they were way off! They thought that the man in the picture was probably jogging through the park and instead of looking at his watch because he was late, he was probably looking at his watch because he was trying to gauge his speed and distance. They were crazy! The man was clearly late for work or for a meeting or something like that. It was ludicrous to think that the man was simply out taking a jog through the park IN HIS BUSINESS SUIT!!

This is when the discussion began to get quite interesting. Some people from the other group were quick to point out the flaws in our logic and some people from our group were quick to point out the flaws in *their* logic. For the most part I kept pretty quiet because I have never been one to speculate. I hate when I don't have all the information!

But some people didn't mind speaking. In fact, it looked as though some people were quite eager to prove the other side wrong. Maria occasionally jumped into the discussion but she seemed to focus mostly on the most vocal people.

She asked Jim, "Why do you think their logic is out of whack? Do you think you have the best description possible?"

Jim eagerly replied, "I just think they are wrong! I'm really not sure what the best description would be but I'm fairly certain that their description is not even close to the best one possible."

Some people were talking, some people were explaining, some people were rationalizing, and some people began to raise their voices (forcing!). And some people were getting a little angry at the other group. They became defensive. Now, I must say that this class was quite accustomed to each other. We had been together for quite a while at that point and most of us were pretty good at pushing the others' buttons. We knew what made the others tick. So there were plenty of smiles and laughs to go along with the bickering! But those (somewhat) personal relationships made the experience that much more realistic because the barrier of stranger passiveness had been shattered long ago with this crowd! Besides that, the students in the class (most of which would consider the others as friends) felt no need to hide their feelings. They were attuned to keeping the classroom experiences real. They were well aware of the fact that each and every one of us would get more out of the program if we kept it real. And so they all did!

This deliberate verisimilitude resulted in some real feelings of hostility and defensiveness. Some of the students were rather open about their feeling of disbelief that the other group thought a different way than they thought.

"How could they be so illogical?"
"How could they think that way?"
"Do they even know what they are thinking?"
"I know they are wrong! I may not be right but I know that they are wrong!"

At one point it got pretty heated until someone from our group yelled out, "Why in the world would a man go jogging through the park in his business suit?!"

Everybody froze. The room was silent and I couldn't even count the number of "What the heck is he talking about?" expressions that I saw on people's faces.

Maria then turned on the overhead projector. Two pictures were revealed…one with the man in the business suit that we saw and the other picture that looked exactly the same as the first except that the man pictured was wearing a jogging suit. That picture was the one given to the other group.

Maria then went back to the blackboard and drew a big circle around the words that were up there.

It's not me, it's you.
I'm not thinking wrong, you are.
I'm not the one being illogical, you are.

These are the thoughts that most of us had throughout the exercise. Few of us stopped to think, "I won't take this personally. I won't attack those that have different views than me. I'll analyze the problem and help to determine the solution."

All too often it is emotion that dictates our actions at a time when logic and resolve should be taking over. And most importantly, we tend to make assumptions about the situation or the other person that may or may not be correct.

"Many of our judgmental attitudes arise from...assumptions we make" (Boyle, 1999, pg. 170). We tend to judge others because we think they have less logic or reasoning than we think we have. We may take their comments personally because we are assuming that they have the exact same information that we have (and why else would they think differently with the same information than because they want to attack us?). Why do we do this? Why do we let things get personal when emotion has little place or use in the discussion? Why do we assume things that we do not know?

Perhaps there is something worse than assumptions. Perhaps we hold on tightly to assumptions because knowing that we don't know something is a rather frightening proposition! Not knowing may be worse than the consequences of assuming (Boyle, pg. 170).

After listening to some new explanations (and some apologies!), Maria strolled to the blackboard and erased **It's Not You, It's Me**. In its place she wrote **It's Nothing Personal!**

Her words became her emphasis: It's not personal. Don't take things so personally. Review the facts. Consider the information. Don't get emotional. After all, it's nothing personal!

After that class I was trying to figure out a way to incorporate the day's lesson into the "discussions" that I occasionally have with my wife. I tried to think of scenarios where I could simply say "It's nothing personal…you are just clearly wrong!" and not get hit in the face with a shoe or end up on Dr. Phil. I couldn't. So I turned to investing.

What would it mean to a trader to keep things from getting personal? Well we have already learned that emotion has little place in the world of investing. So instead of thinking about what is at stake with investing, perhaps we should focus on the game of investing. Don't make it personal. Money isn't personal. Money doesn't care. So why should you?

In other words, trade as if you are playing a game. Pretend that you are trading points or chips instead of money. Follow your time tested rules with no emotion and forget about everything else!

Of course, this is a lot easier said than done. Money runs this world. Everything is money. You couldn't just possibly forget that you are using real money even though the results of your actions could result in you not being able to drive a car or live in a house, right? Exactly!

The key is to understand that money is not changing hands until it is changing hands. If your stock goes up, your buying power has not changed…until you sell. Likewise, if your stock goes down, your buying power has not changed either. You can still buy everything you could have bought the day before you looked in the newspaper to find your Motorola stock lose 25%. You have not lost anything yet! So stop counting dollars with every change of the market. Stop worrying about the dollars you are losing or gaining and start playing your game (at the very least until you sell).

Simply pretend that it is not money and play your game. Pretend that your account represents points scored instead of dollars. This is really the key to true stressfree trading. If you stick to your game plan as mentioned in the previous chapters and pretend that you are playing with points instead of money, your stress level will crash. It will be the Great Depression of your stress market! Not only that, your profits will soar because you won't be tempted to let emotions ruin your game.

Do you remember when Rocky fought Apollo Creed at the end of Rocky 3? Of course, they didn't show us what happened after they began their private boxing match but I can bet that Rocky would have won the match. He would have won as long as he put on his game face and did not allow his friendship with Apollo to get in the way of his performance. After all, he was a professional boxer. There are no friends in the ring even when there is nobody watching and no money is involved! I mean, think about how successful Michael Jordan would have been had he let his emotions get in the way of his basketball performance. Do you think he would have won as much if he didn't play his game every time he played one of his friends? He had Charles Barkleys on almost every team…he would have been a complete failure!

But he wasn't. He was a professional basketball player. He did not let emotions get in the way of his performance. He didn't let it get personal. He always played his game. He NEVER relented. He never said, "Well maybe this game I'll go easy on Charles because he is my friend". No way! He always stuck to his gameplan and he was one of the most successful basketball players ever. He was a professional. He succeeded.

You can do the same thing with trading. Don't let it get personal. Stick to your game plan. Be a professional. Succeed!

Think about it. No more will you be wasting your time watching the quotes in the middle of the trading day and thinking, "Wow! I have just made enough to buy a new car!" or "Ugh, I've just lost all my money and won't be able to afford those Christmas presents I was going to buy for my family".

No one can succeed like this (without getting an ulcer, anyway). This kind of trading is emotionally draining, and you won't last very long. But perhaps most of all, you'll just downright hate it. This was me in my early days. I would be so down when I checked my quotes throughout the day only to find I had ultimately lost $500. And then the next day I was the life of the party because my quotes showed that I was up $500!

Even if I could have been successful trading this way I would have hated it. I would have gotten sick and I would have given up pretty early on. It wouldn't have been worth it.

Reports came out this morning that showed that, for the first time in the history of this country, more than half of all the households in America own stock (whether individually or in a retirement account). This is great but I wonder how many of those people are enjoying themselves. That number really would be closer to 70% if people knew how to trade without the stress.

How many people would own stocks if they did it the way I have been doing it? With my low risk/high reward system I check the charts at the end of the day in five minutes and that's it. I simply ask myself the questions that I have set up to be a part of my trading plan:

1. Should I buy according to my rules

2. Should I sell according to my rules

3. Should I hold according to my rules

And that is it! No stress. No wondering if I'm losing or gaining. No ulcers. I'm just playing my game. I've got six more points today than I had yesterday...now what do I do with them? And the best part is that my rules stipulate that I give myself only ten seconds to answer each of the questions above. I'm no longer a trader. I'm a rule follower (why do you think I have all this time to write books?)!

One thing that I found consistent with many prominent traders was their interest in following Market Wizards I and II. They never really saw the markets as a cash box but simply as a way of operating a business or playing a game. The name of their business (or game) was Follow The Rules To Score Points. It's just not possible to become a successful and stressfree trader if you view every single tick in the market as money in or out of your pocket. You can't win the game if you take it personally!

The general consensus among the top traders today is that emotions and stress are the most potent destroyers of successful trading. It is also logical to assume that making and losing money is stressful. It is a stressful business. Money equals stress. So logic would dictate that in order to be a highly successful trader you need to eliminate the stress. You need to eliminate the emotions. You won't become stressed about money if you aren't using money! You'll be scoring points, gaining chips, winning a game. You won't be constantly gaining and losing money. If money is so stressful then simply remove it from the equation!

How do you do this? Simple. Just follow your rules without prejudice or passion. Become a rule follower.

If you ever read just one more book on the stock market then please let it be *How I Made $2,000,000 In The Stock Market* by Nicolas Darvas (1986).

I love this book so much because when you have read it as many times as I have (over fifty times) you begin to realize just how well this gentleman turned his trading around from an emotional losing trader into a robotic, disciplined, money-generating machine. Besides following the rules that I have laid out in the previous chapters, Mr. Darvas did one thing extraordinarily well: He removed emotion from his trading. He became a rule follower. He established his rules and got to a point where no decisions (stress-inducers) had to be made. When his rules told him to buy, he bought. When his rules told him to sell, he sold. When his rules told him to hold, he held. He did not think about how much money he could gain or lose with that non-decision. He simply followed his rules, played his game, took money out of the equation, and became incredibly successful…and rich!

It made no difference to him whether the buy was for $5,000 or $50,000. It was all the same to him. It was just a game and he followed his rules. He stopped counting money and flawlessly followed his game plan. This is all well and good in theory, you say?

Let me share with you one situation with Mr. Darvas that had a profound and ever-lasting effect on my trading:

In one trade Mr. Darvas bought $350,000 of a share at $53 1/2. The share then climbed to over $100 and his broker sent him a telegram with the message: Profits now $250,000. Up to that point, Mr. Darvas had completely forgotten about the paper profits that had been building up. He was just playing his game and following his rules. He knew at that point that he could sell out and be rich for life (this was in the 1950's!). His rules told him not to sell. If he continued doing what he had been doing he could miss out on a huge win, right? Every single fiber in his body was telling him to abandon his rules and sell. After all, if he sold out wouldn't he have won the game? Wasn't the point of the game to become rich? Don't quite know how to answer that?

Mr. Darvas didn't know the answer either! So he walked around Paris trying to work out what to do. For the first time in a while he pondered. He thought about what to do. He thought about forgetting his game and becoming rich. Shall I sell and make the sure profit? Shall I break my rules just this one time because of the obvious gain? Is the game more important? Are the rules more important? Or is the money more important?

Back and forth in his mind the answers to those questions went. He couldn't come to a decision as quickly as he would have liked. After all, he was already kind of breaking his rules by even considering breaking his rules, right!?

As you may have guessed if you have ever heard of Nicolas Darvas, he stuck to his rules and decided not to sell. He played his game. After all, he wasn't playing with money. He was playing with points! And the rules were more important than the points! It was the hardest non-decision of his life. But because he truly believed in his principles he stuck to his game and did not alter. He didn't budge even with hundreds of thousands of dollars being waived in his face.

Of course, his rules worked out even better than he could have ever dreamed. Over the course of the next few weeks his shares climbed even higher. By the time his rules told him to sell, he made even more money than he would have had he broken his rules a few weeks prior. He won that game. But not because he made more money. No way! He won that game because he stuck to his rules. He did not give in to temptation. He did not allow emotions, stress, or money dictate how he was going to play *his* game.

Had he been constantly watching the ticks day in and day out he probably would have gotten out a great deal earlier. He would have made less money. Very few people would have had the nerve to stay in as long as he did and make as much as he did. But he didn't need nerve. He just needed his rules!

So theory is all well and good but reality is much more powerful. Don't just look at the theory. Look at the examples of how the theory worked. Follow in the footsteps of Mr. Darvas and play your game!

Most traders on Wall Street know the old sayings:

1. "Cut your losses"
2. "Let your profits run"
3. "Trade with the trend"
4. blah, blah, blah, blah

Of course, the good traders know that last one better than the first three! In the heat of battle you need to have a powerful ally. And trust me, you don't want those first three sayings to be your allies. You'll get creamed! Use your rules. You'll be comfortable. You won't be stressed. You won't need to make decisions. You won't waste your time. You won't lose!

Occasionally I still come to a situation where I want to bend my rules. "Just this one time," I'll say to myself. I'll try to convince myself that it will be worth it just this one time. But then I'll remember Nicolas Darvas.

I have gathered enough experience to realize that I can NEVER break my rules. Not once. Not one trade. No exceptions. And the only way I have been able to stick to this plan is by eliminating money from the equation. Making it impersonal. Making it a game. After all, who cares if I lose a few points in this game?! What is the best part about playing a game? Winning…maybe. Losing…probably not. Playing…you bet! There is always a chance that you will lose a game but you agree to play anyway because playing is fun! Sure, winning is nice. But playing is the best part.

So what exactly separates the winners from the losers? I really have a hard time believing that it is knowledge or intelligence. I have seen too many exceptions to that theory to understand that it has to be something else. So what is it? Luck? I really hope not! It would really be rather pointless for anybody to play if luck was the main thing that separated the winners from the losers. At that rate we may as well all play the card game War!

No, I firmly believe that what truly separates the winners from the losers is the ability to follow your rules WITHOUT EXCEPTION! There is an entire spectrum of trading success. Those at the top of the spectrum are those who never break their rules. Those at the bottom are people who don't even have any rules to follow. They just wing it or follow the guidance of someone who is trying to make money off of them. Those in the middle may have a gameplan but will break their rules on occasion. Sometimes I will come across a trader who has a set of rules and follows it most of the time. That trader will be marginally successful but just can't understand why (s)he is not at the top. Well, it has become rather obvious to me over the years that those people are on the right track. They just need to eliminate emotions and money from the equation entirely…and not just when it is convenient for them. They need to ALWAYS follow their rules.

Isn't that what "stressfree" means? For those of you who are parents, I'll bet you are nodding in agreement. Just think about a world where you don't have to make any hard decisions at all, ever. Imagine a world where the only decisions you have to make are which game to play with your kids and what food you are having for dinner. Boring, you say? Yes…but it would also be STRESSFREE! Not having to make decisions is the basis for stressfree trading.

Very few traders have the discipline to do this. Very few traders are at the top of that spectrum. Very few traders can honestly tell themselves, "It's nothing personal"!

8

To Be a Successful Trader, Don't Be a Successful Trader

When I returned home from class one night I found my wife asleep on the couch with the television remote control in one hand and a book that she was reading at the time in the other hand. I couldn't help but think about how great her balance must be to be able to hold those two items in her hand AS SHE SLEPT!

That got me thinking about what kind of balance she had in her life at the time. She was a very successful developmental therapist for small children, a successful wife, a successful mother, a Reiki therapist, and a new student in a PhD program. Not only that, she evidently had some mystic balancing power that enabled her to not drop things that she was holding onto even while falling into a deep sleep!

Then I started to think about the balance that I had in my life. One thing that I realized that night was that there was a very specific reason as to why I had begun the Applied Behavioral Science program in the first place. I needed balance. Whether it was on the forefront of my mind or somewhere deep in the subconscious, I knew that there was something out of balance in my life. It wasn't anything that I could necessarily pinpoint at the time but I knew that an education in the field of human behavior may give me a small clue.

That night I realized that the one thing that was a little out of place in my life was purpose. I was doing well by most standards. I was staying home to raise my two children (I now have been blessed with a third!), I ran a somewhat successful business (although still a fraction of the success of my wife's business), I had one book published with a second being considered by publishers, and I played basketball every Sunday morning. Life was grand! But I needed a purpose to bring everything together. I needed a source of energy that could fuel all of these "successes". And I figured an education in the field of human behavior was the answer.

That night I also realized that I was well on my way towards that balance that I had craved, that was necessary for me to continue feeling good about my life's endeavors. The education was working!

I then remembered something that Maria had taught us about balance in one's life. She used the text from Stephen Covey's Seventh Habit to describe the one thing that would act as the glue to make all the pieces of your life's puzzle fit together; he referred to it as sharpening the saw (Covey, pg. 287). The paradigm that Covey uses is the one that finds one person sawing a tree in the forest. Another person walks by and finds the first drenched in perspiration. The second person asks the first why he looks so exhausted and the first replies that he had been sawing the tree for several hours and that it was very hard work. The second person asks the first why he doesn't sharpen his saw in order to make the work go much easier and faster (because after that much constant sawing the saw must have been terribly dull). The first person explained that he had no time to sharpen his saw because he was so busy sawing that tree! (Covey, pg. 287)

Before I started the ABS program I felt like that person sawing the tree. I had so many responsibilities and I really felt as though I was succeeding at all of them. But I was told (by something inside me as opposed to a person walking by) that I needed something to pull everything together. I needed balance.

So that night as I watched my wife performing her balancing act I realized that I was currently sharpening my saw. I was going to school to learn about how to be a more efficient and effective person. I was gaining balance.

It's funny how things work out because during the next class the students were given a survey form by Maria. Occasionally the school wanted to know how the program was going. They wanted to know if the students felt as excited about the results of the program as the creators of it did!

The last question of the survey asked if there was anything that I would change about the program if I could. I began to write a great deal about how the lessons learned were wonderful but that I felt as though the subtlety of the manner in which they were learned could be changed. In other words, I knew that I had learned the lessons that were presented to me but I was concerned that other students may have missed some of the lessons because they weren't taught in a straightforward format. I was a thinker. I would think for hours after each class. And I often began to understand the true lessons after hours and days of heavy thinking and pondering. Did other students have as much time to invest in the subjects as I had? Did they all learn as much as I did? Or did they miss things that I would have missed had I not put so much thought and energy into deciphering the messages taught?

Ultimately I ended up crossing out what I had written because I realized that it may have been necessary for me to think as much as I did only because I was a slow learner. Perhaps the others learned the lessons with a little less effort. I concluded that the program was being taught perfectly because the students could put as much effort and thought into the program that was necessary for them to understand the lessons.

Of course, I was a little anxious to broach the subject with Maria after the surveys had all been completed. I asked her what she thought about the way the program was set up and if it would be easier to teach the subjects in a more traditional manner. Her response was indicative of why I loved the program so much!

She asked if I had seen the movie *The Sixth Sense*. After replying that I had seen the movie, she asked if I enjoyed the "trick" ending. I told her it was one of my favorite movies and that I loved the trick ending and all the little twists that constantly kept you on your toes because it really kept your attention and made you think throughout the entire movie. She then got a little smile on her face and asked if I thought I would have liked the movie as much if all those tricks and twists were revealed to me at the beginning of the film.

"Of course not," I replied. "It wouldn't have made me think as much if I was told everything before anything happened. Half the fun of the movie would have been gone!"

Maria just smiled and looked at the rest of the class, who seemed to understand before I even asked the questions. The average adult human being loves to figure things out for themselves. They feel a sense of accomplishment when they complete a task themselves. They are less motivated when they are simply told what to do.

And to not break precedent, the little discussion that we had brought us right into the next section of the program that dealt with management and leadership (these little self discoveries always seemed to offer Maria a perfect transition into the next section of the program). Maria immediately began to explain the "Immaturity-Maturity Theory" of management by Chris Argyris (Hersey, 2001, pg. 65). The basic theory is that people generally mature as they age. They go from being passive to active; dependant to independent; understanding only the present to understanding the past and future as well; and so on and so forth (Hersey, pg. 65).

So the fact that I enjoyed the Sixth Sense because it offered me an opportunity to discover the plot for myself was one example of how I was more active and less passive. In my immature years, I would have been just as satisfied, if not more so, to have my parents explain the movie to me instead of me trying to figure it out for myself. Similarly, the students in the ABS program seemed to really appreciate what they were learning. They enjoyed the fact that they were figuring out things on their own. The material wasn't simply told to them. They truly learned the lessons (as opposed to being told the lessons). We were all being taught in a mature way!

This was the balance that I had been seeking. I was sharpening my saw! I wasn't going to school just to get a degree or just to enhance my resume. I was trying to learn how to balance my life. That was my goal for the program…and it was working wonderfully.

What I have come to realize after that "Immaturity-Maturity" class was that I needed to find balance but I needed to find it myself. I couldn't be told by someone else to have balance in my life. I could be guided toward that discovery by the teachings of Maria and Stephen Covey and others but it was important for me to truly learn that concept myself. And, like with the Sixth Sense, it would be more fun that way, too!

So it is no wonder that I firmly believe that balance is the catalyst necessary to become a successful trader (and person?!). Let's face it, trading has traditionally been viewed as a rather stressful activity. As I stated last chapter, you must do whatever you can to eliminate as much of that stress as possible. I have never met a successful trader that was constantly stressed. Usually, it is quite the opposite. Most of the highly successful traders that I have spoken with are rather laid back in their trading approach. They seemed very relaxed and confident. I have no doubts that these characteristics are what helped to mold and form those traders into the successes they are today.

But what does this mean? Does this mean that you have to not care? Does this mean that you have to be able to throw caution into the wind? Does this mean that you have to be passionless about trading? Well, sort of…

After reading *Market Wizards* (Swager) I found that one common factor picked up on all the best traders was their ability to disassociate themselves with the market action. It really was as if they didn't care. They seemed to never be concerned about their positions. Considering that some of these traders had millions of dollars on the line, I find that fact almost unbelievable! How could they possibly not care? How could they continue to have a smile on their faces through thick and thin? After all, most of the (unsuccessful) traders I knew (including myself in the early on) would get over anxious and rather excited when they only had a couple hundred dollars to lose.

But one thing that I discovered over the years was that my success increased exponentially once I began to spend less time trying to control the market (by watching it every few minutes and trying to will it to go my way). I would stare at that quote machine and end of day graphs all the time. I couldn't stop. It reminded me of when my wife was in labor. I could not take my eyes off of that statistics machine (you know which one I'm talking about if you are a husband of someone in labor…the one that shows the strength of the contractions and the heart rate of the mother and child). My eyes were glued to that screen. I was obsessed! But what should I have been paying attention to? Certainly not that stupid machine that told me how my wife was probably feeling. I should have been paying attention to her! I remember telling her, "You should be in pain now, your contraction number is 72!"

Then I would get a look like I was the stupidest, most insensitive person in the world! Like, duh! I was paying attention to the wrong things. I was looking at a machine to tell me how my wife was feeling instead of looking at and talking to her. But that is what husbands do, right!?

Well, that is what I did as an early trader. I was looking at the numbers and the machines and the newspapers. After all, that is what traders do, right!?

RIGHT!!

But what I am here to tell you is that you don't want to be a trader. You want to be a successful trader. And in order to be a successful trader, you can't be a trader (got it?)!

What I mean is you need balance. Trading needs to be just one small thing on your plate. It needs to be the little dinner roll next to your steak, potatoes, corn, and salad. It's just one small part of the meal. Your plate needs balance! Just imagine if all you had on that plate was that little dinner roll. You wouldn't be able to focus on anything else. You would just keep staring at that dinner roll. You would pray that that dinner roll will fill you up. You would hope to no end that that dinner roll would be so good that it would be enough to satisfy you. Unfortunately, I can't think of a dinner roll on this planet that would be enough to satisfy my dinner needs!

Don't let trading be the only thing in your life. Once I realized this, I took up basketball, writing, jogging, tennis, school, computers, photography, and a world of other things that make up life. I knew that I needed to take my total focus away from the markets. I needed a life!

The great thing is that, along with the quality of my life improving by leaps and bounds, the results of my trading also skyrocketed. I was doing better than I ever thought I could do simply by applying the principles I mentioned in these chapters. I worked less and gained more. What could be grander!

So to review, how can the top traders keep it so cool when the risks and stakes are so high? What works?

1. They decided a long time ago to take responsibility and find out what works

2. They have a system that fits them perfectly

3. They plan every trade down to the finest detail by sticking to their rules. They never compromise those rules ever, for any reason. They stick to their rules no matter what

4. They put the ground work into their system and continue to grow and learn. They don't stop learning because they know that they knowledge they have is wonderful for the time being but in order to stay successful they need to keep up with the ever-changing economy

5. They have complete confidence in their system and they flawlessly execute it

6. They view trading as a game and stopped counting money a long time ago. Most top traders are now rather wealthy so if they no longer enjoyed their game, they would have retired

7. They learned a long time ago that they can't control the markets. They don't constantly watch those machines and numbers. They focus on the important things in life and realize that balance is the key to success.

Trading really is no different than any other aspect of your life. I know it sounds obvious but whenever you focus on only one thing in life, the other things seem to suffer. This is just common sense. If your total focus is on one point then the importance of every single little dip and peak becomes extremely exaggerated. This kind of peak and valley emotional trading will not only ruin your trading results but may in fact leave you destroyed as a person, too.

In order to be a successful trader, you need to learn how to take time away from trading. You need to learn how to not be a trader! Re-charge those batteries and gain a little perspective. I remember my first few years as a trader. I would spend all day, night, weekends, and holidays reading, studying, staring at the charts, trying different systems, etc. Frankly I wouldn't wish it upon my worst enemies. Trading is stressful. Imagine doing nothing but trading! I would certainly have kept my life more balanced had I known all along. I learned a lot in those times but I was miserable. Remember, work hard and play hard…not work hard and then work some more.

The stresses of trading are bad enough without making it your only focus. If you have nothing to "go home to" and you have no other interests, then the world of investing is going to eat you alive. Instead of evaluating your overall performance in the market every day or every week, try writing a ten year business plan or list of goals for your investing endeavors. When you look at it in the big picture, you will be more apt to enjoy yourself in the meantime. But if you focus on hourly or daily goals, you won't have much energy to do much of anything else.

Find your purpose and gain balance in your life. Trading should just be a small piece of that puzzle. Much like the secret to success of other jobs, work hard while you are on the job but be disciplined enough to switch off after you punch out and live your life. Don't take your stresses home with you. Schedule in your trading. Don't schedule in your life!

Some of my very best trades over the years were the ones where I would place a buy order on a stock and leave my broker with the stop loss order. I would then go on vacation or a sabbatical for months at a time without so much as giving the stocks a single thought. I would come back home to find that my system once again worked perfectly and my shares jumped 40%. It really never ceases to amaze me just how simple (and stressfree!) successful trading can be.

I guess you just have to ask yourself why you are working so hard now, whether it be in the stock market or at your 9 to 5 job. If you are like me, you are working hard so that you can earn time; time to be with your family and time to spend doing the things that you really enjoy doing. So how can you accomplish that goal of time if you do nothing but spend every minute of every day looking at the charts and agonizing over your trading?

It's kind of like the story of the small town Mexican fisherman that I heard in one of my classes. You've all heard this one before, right?

It begins with a fisherman living in a small coastal town in Mexico. He wakes up around noon every day to go out fishing. He only fishes for a couple hours each day…just enough to ensure that he can sell enough to take care of the basic needs and wants of his family. After returning from his work in the early afternoon he typically will play with his children for a couple of hours before taking an evening siesta with his wife. Upon waking, he and his family have a grand supper full of fresh fish, rolls, beans, and corn. After supper he tucks his wife and children into bed and meets up with his buddies at the tavern down the street. He drinks wine and plays his guitar with his friends into the wee hours of the night. He grabs a lemon ice on his way home and sleeps until noon the next day…

Then one day a cruise ship docks in a nearby port for a few hours in order to refuel. A wealthy American businessman exits the ship and decides to take a stroll down the streets of this small Mexican town. He finds the fisherman walking down the street carrying two large bags of fish that he had caught that day. The wealthy businessman strikes up a conversation with the fisherman and finds out that all the fisherman in this small Mexican town have a similar schedule. They work only a couple hours a day and they never think anything of it. "Let me show you how to really make it big," says the businessman to the small town fisherman.

"You could really clean up. We could work together to become the premier fishery in the region. We could get several boats and eventually be the only game in town. Then I could bring you to New York and show you how to start your own American company. You could branch out and have several successful fisheries. Then you could release your own IPO and make millions!"

"How long will this take?" asked the small town fisherman.

"Probably no more than 20 years," replied the wealthy American businessman.

"Then what do I do?" asked the small town fisherman.

"Well then the fun really starts!" replied the wealthy American businessman. "You could retire a wealthy man and do all the things you have ever dreamed of. You could do anything you want. What is your idea of heaven, because it could be yours!"

"Let's see...my idea of heaven," said the small town fisherman, "would be to sleep in until noon, go out fishing for a couple of hours, come home and play with my kids in the sun. Then I would take a siesta with my wife and wake up in the evening to a grand feast. I would then love to sip wine with my buddies all night while playing my guitar..."

The Mexican fisherman wasn't deliberately trying to be a smartass. He just truly wondered if the American businessman knew what wealth really meant. The fisherman wasn't sure if the businessman knew why he was working...what his purpose was.

What do you think is the true measure of a person's wealth? Life is funny. If we aren't careful, we get what we wish for...we just have to make sure we really put some time and energy into determining exactly what it is that we want. The point is, figure out what you want before you start working towards your goals. Don't do the work if you have no idea how to measure your success. The small town fisherman knew exactly what he wanted and he did exactly what was necessary to fulfill his dreams and desires. He was, by all accounts, a very wealthy man. And he only worked two hours a day!

This reminds me of another of Covey's Habits: Begin With The End In Mind (Covey, pg. 97). In other words, know exactly what it is you are working for. Don't just work and hope that you'll get something good out of it. Know what your goals are, if for no other reason than to be able to recognize them when you achieve them. It's funny. Sometimes I see people wandering around their lives thinking they need to do things a certain way. They have been brainwashed to believe that they need to follow a certain pattern. But they don't! That's the beauty of this world. You make your rules!!

Trading is funny, too. It's a weird way to make money. It's almost like interest…you can make money by not doing anything (or much of anything). Some people would almost feel guilty about this. Some people think that they should work forty or fifty hours a week in order to earn their paycheck. Again, they get caught up in believing these traditionalist views. They don't know any better.

But my hope for you is that by reading these ideas you will begin to know better! Think about it for a minute. Let's say that you buy $50,000 worth of stock at $50 and sell one year later at $200 (because that is what your rules and your system told you to do). You have just made $150,000 profit (minus fees if applicable). Amazingly, it only took about sixty minutes to earn this money. You simply spent about a minute every other day or so making sure that you followed your rules. What else was there to do?

The funny thing is that most people would have had a difficult time doing this. Some may feel guilty. Others would get too antsy. And yet others would feel stressed when the price reached $70 because they would want to break their rules and sell then for the sure profit. Unfortunately, all of these people would have missed out on the full $150,000. The balanced trader would have been spending his time wisely that year and followed his/her rules without exception. (S)he would have been fishing or hiking or swimming or playing basketball while the others were sweating over the daily numbers.

So keep it in perspective. Realize that you have no way of controlling the prices. You'll find yourself itching for something to do (because following your rules only takes about one minute per day) so find some other interests. Here is something simple you can do in order to ensure that you are not spending too much time managing your trades: Get yourself a good kitchen timer and set it to fifteen minutes every morning when you wake up. Start it every time you think about your trades (yes, think!) and every time you look at the newspaper or read the charts. Then stop it every time you stop doing those things. If the bell rings at any point before you go to bed every night, you are spending too much time trying to manage your trades. You are trying to see something that just does not exist.

So just remember that successful trading is:

- Boring
- Effortless
- Easy
- Stressfree

Successful trading will happen to you. Just follow the rules outlined in these chapters, determine your path, and stick to it! Of course, this is not going to happen overnight. You have to make these rules your habits. Habits are something that you do without thought. You won't have to refer to this book once these rules become habits. You will just do them automatically. It will take time, but I guarantee you the results will be well worth it. At the very least you'll save money on antacid!

Section II

The Trading Programs

9

Trading Programs for the Adult Learner

The first section of this book focused on the theories of successful trading. What do you have to do in order to be successful? What do you have to change?

This section of the book will focus on two very useable, very manageable trading programs that can be implemented by almost anyone. In fact, they are written for the average adult learner. Throughout my studies I have learned a few things about what it means to be an average adult learner. You see, an adult learner is different than a child learner. For a child learner, the teacher must teach the lessons while externally motivating the youngster (if you have kids you know what I mean…"just sit down on the potty for three minutes and I'll give you a sticker or a treat"). A child generally wants to see what the reward is before completing the task.

Teaching an adult learner is a whole different ballgame! Adult learners tend to be motivated from within. Sure, the rewards of money and success and status all come in to play but the real motivating factor to an adult who is faced with learning something new is what comes from within. Adult learners can think of their own reasons for learning a new task. They understand the rewards without having to be told what the rewards are. They motivate themselves and they expect to be given the opportunity to learn at their own pace and with their own goals in mind.

These two trading programs are specifically designed for just such an adult learner. They will provide guidance but you will be able to fully understand the rewards yourself. You won't need me to tell you! And you can spend as much time learning these programs and integrating them with your own trading style as you wish. This is not a "Learn How To Trade In Nine Days" type of program. This is more of a "Learn How To Trade At Your Pace" type of program.

But before we get to the programs, perhaps we should recap the secrets of the successful and stressfree trader. So let us take a look at a short Q & A session (fun!).

Q1) How can I become a successful trader with lots of spare time and a well balanced life?

A1) View trading as a game in term of points. Money is stressful so remove it from the equation.

Q2) But how do I do this?

A2) You have to really have total belief in yourself and your system.

Q3) How do I get this?

A3) Do the ground work on your system and yourself. Keep working towards perfection and don't be afraid of failures along the way. Sometimes failure is the best teacher and most powerful motivator around.

Q4) What kind of work...how do I work towards perfection?

A4) Plan for every eventuality in every trade. If you missed one the first time, add it to your list and don't miss it again. Be like the Boy Scouts. And most importantly, develop the discipline to follow your plan without exception.

Q5) How do I plan a trade and have confidence in this plan?

A5) Either start from scratch and learn enough to build your own system or find a system that fits your personality as a trader (and don't be afraid to tweak it in order to make it YOUR plan).

Q6) How do I go about finding such a system?

A6) Read the next two chapters to learn two systems that have helped thousands of people! If neither of those two systems work for you then visit our websites at www.yourinvestmentclub.com or www.stressfree-trading.com to find some more systems.[1]

Before deciding on your system, make sure you reread the first section of this book so that you are well versed in the secrets of successful trading. Remember that the idea is to make the process stressfree!

Some clichés to look out for:

- Let your profits run
- Cut your losses
- Follow your rules (you have to really know what this means so if you skipped over the first section, make sure you go back and read it before continuing!)

Also be sure to watch out for some of the really bad advice that is out there today including:

- You can never go broke taking a profit
- Buy a good stock and forget about it (buy and hold theory)
- Buy low and sell high

---

1.   One focusing on investment education and the other on investment programs.

Successful and stressfree trading goes well beyond these ancient quotes and sayings. So don't just buy a good stock and hold on to it…buy a good stock and hold on to it *when your rules tell you to hold on to it*!

95% of the people who try to get into trading fail the first year. Some people seem to be naturally better at trading then others. But I firmly believe that anyone can be a successful trader. They just have to follow the simple rules outlined in the preceeding chapters and follow their rules.

I have taken these very principles and used them over the years to help me develop several trading systems that can be used by just about any type of trader. I have included two of these systems in this book. Again, make sure you understand the principles of successful and stressfree trading before you adopt the following systems.

The reason that I have decided to include these two systems in this book was because I believe that the Weekly Small Cap Trading System and the 1-2-3 Trading System are my two most straightforward program that are the simplest to utilize no matter what your trading experience may be.

You have just learned the theory behind becoming a successful and stressfree trader. Now are you ready to apply some of the knowledge towards trading? Remember, the most important aspects of successful and stressfree trading are developing a plan that you fully believe in and then sticking to that plan without exception. So these two trading systems that I have developed should give you a great starting point towards developing the trading system that is perfectly tailored to your needs and ideals as an investor. At some points, you may think you are reading a workbook. That's good! Write all over these pages (after all, you can always purchase several more copies to keep in pristine condition!). These systems are designed to be worked through by you.

Plus, after gaining a small understanding about adult behavior and the different (complex!) learning styles that adults possess through my Adult Behavior Studies program, these two systems seem to be perfectly tailored to the adult learner!!

Let me explain. The average adult learner seems to be less dependant upon external motivators when it comes to learning something new (National-Louis, 1999, pg. 15). However, this certainly does not mean that the average adult learner does not need any help. Quite the contrary! The adult learner will enlist the help of others as a source of knowledge, reference, understanding, and encouragement (National-Louis, pg. 37). Well, these two trading systems on the following pages take those principles to heart. They will show you the path towards developing your system. You could even use these systems to make actual trades (and be quite successful along the way!) while you are learning about yourself as a trader. But they are not pushy. Again, this is not a Learn-In-14-Days investment program. You are an adult learner and that means that you get to learn it your way (finally, a reward for sitting through four years of high school history class lectures)!

These systems can be your references. Go ahead and refer back to them when you are making your own trades. Or simply follow them to a tee if you feel your trading style is perfectly reflected by the nuances of these programs.

One more thing about the average adult learner: Don't stop! What I have learned through my studies is that adults really need to feel success and then scrutinize every last drop of it before they feel comfortable in performing the same task. In other words, if they do a job and know that they are doing it well, they will continue to do it. So for goodness' sake, if you realize the potential success of your system then do not stop trading with it! Feedback and follow-up will be crucial elements in your development of your system. After all, you are a learner. And adult learners need to evaluate their performance if they are to feel comfortable with continuing the learning process (National-Louis, pg. 38). You are not a child (or at least you likely won't be for long!) so you are not going to simply use the system, achieve the results, and never think about it again. Right?!

Of course not! You are going to use this system, integrate it into your trading style, develop it as you go along at your own pace, and evaluate the process until you are comfortable enough with your program and have enough faith in it so that you never break your rules and you begin to trade sans stress.

So use these systems and use them wisely…by developing your rules and sticking to them no matter what!

10
The 1-2-3 Trading Signal

The 1-2-3 Trading Signal if really funny because once you train your eyes to see the patterns, you will see them everywhere! At first you will be so excited…"Hey, there it is; the 1-2-3 Trading Signal just like the book said!"

But eventually you will get to the point where spotting them becomes ordinary and acting upon them becomes habit. Of course, no pattern can be 100% successful (or else trading would be no fun, right?) but this is by far the most accurate and profitable pattern I have seen over the years. If you want to become an expert in one chart pattern, this is probably the one you will want to focus on!

Now as I mentioned earlier, you will likely want to develop this system yourself and integrate into your own trading program and rules. One of the reasons why this pattern is a good one to start with is because it is about 95% objective. Once you become an expert using this system, you will likely introduce a slight subjective analysis of the data. That's the idea! But for the sake of this book, I will only focus on the purely objective aspects of this pattern.

So what are the objectives here? What is it you want to learn from this system? Let me give you a pre-summary. You'll learn:

- what exactly the 1-2-3 pattern is
- which charts and time frames exist for the pattern
- the entry "trick"
- the exit

That's it! But before we begin let me tell you how I still use this pattern. I really like to keep my eyes on the 1-2-3 patterns in very oversold/overbought markets, especially on the stock indices and the futures market. And although this method is extremely profitable when used to trade the big cap stocks, I have actually tailored this method to go along with a momentum trading program I developed. Again, most of you will want to develop your own program with guidance from this one.

If you happen to be a pure stock trader, then use the 1-2-3 to determine trend changes on the major indices and keep your eye open to spot them on the stocks you are following.

If you are a futures trader as well then I would seriously consider not only looking for 1-2-3 patterns as to major moves but also adopting this into a complete trading system. For more on this subject, take a look at the web links and recommended reading lists at the conclusion of this book.

So what exactly is a 1-2-3 pattern? That is a good question that is best answered by looking at some charts!

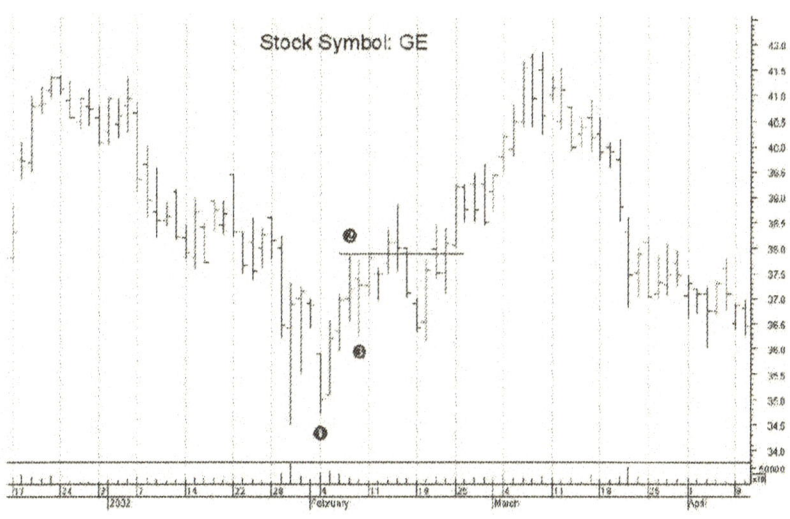

Above is simply a daily bar chart of the stock for the big blue chip US General Electric. The stock symbol is GE.

Clearly marked is the 1-2-3 pattern that evolved in February of last year. This is a great example of a 1-2-3 buy pattern. It is a bottom, a correction, a retest that does not go beyond the original bottom. It is then a rebound beyond the correction. Phew...that was a mouthful! But it is really simple when you look at the chart. Take a look at it again and keep your eyes at Point 1.

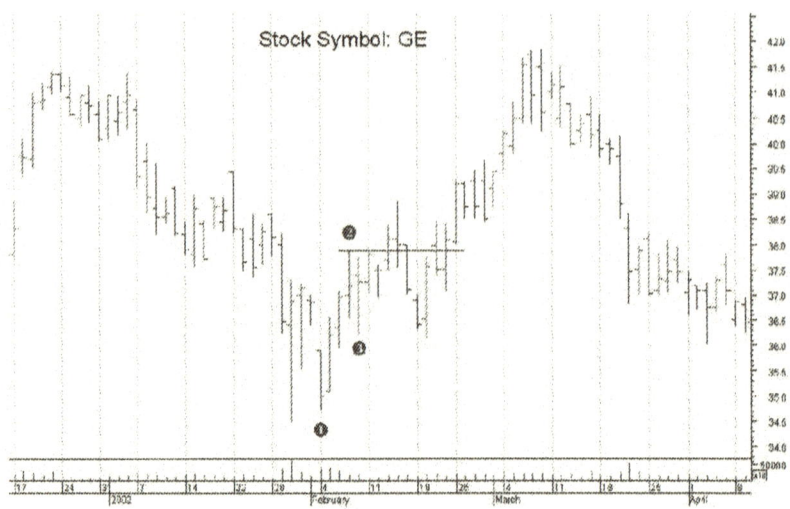

Point 1 represents the bottom. Point 2 is the correction. And Point 3 is the retest. Point 3 is the key because it DOES NOT GO BEYOND Point 1. If it does then all bets are off. In other words, if Point 3 does go beyond Point 1 then you wouldn't be looking at a simple 1-2-3 buy pattern! Just take a look at the chart again and feast your eyes on that number 3 point. You'll see that the pattern of this stock was to dip down to Point 3, then rebound up to Point 2, only to fall back down a little to Point 3. That Point 3 may look low (to most investors who are anxious!) but it will not go below Point 1 (the bottom point). Again, if it does then move on and find something else!

Look at it like this: Try to find a pattern where the ticks have a bottom then a top then a bottom (but not as low as the first bottom). So you'll see this down, up, down pattern and want to buy when it goes back up to the first up. If it never does, then you just don't buy![1]

Once you have a valid 1-2-3 pattern then you would place your buy order in at the **breakout** of the number two point on the pattern. I know that sounds complicated but I will show you what I mean. And once you grasp these basic fundamentals of the pattern then I promise you will see these everywhere.

Take a look at the following chart and notice the peaks and valleys associated with Point 2.

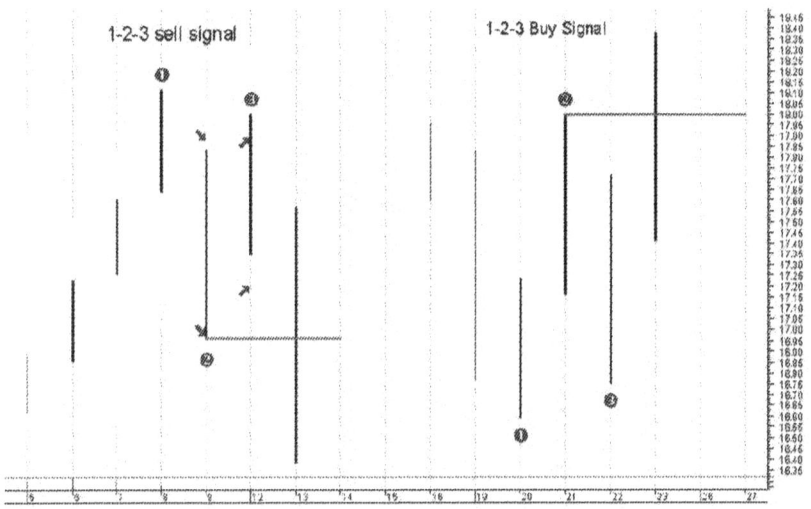

What do you notice? You are keeping your eye on that Point 2, right? If so then you probably are seeing the buying and selling patterns. To illustrate the point, let's do a simple exercise that will help you understand the fundamentals of this system (I may have men-

---

1. A sell order using the 1-2-3 signal would then be the reverse pattern (up, down, up, and then sell when it hits the first down). We will primarily focus on buy orders using the 1-2-3 signal because there are several legitimate exit routes once you have bought.

tioned that this section will read like a school workbook, didn't I?!).
This exercise is loads of fun:

1. Get a blank piece of paper and a pen

2. Starting at the top left hand corner draw a diagonal line to the center of the page

3. Mark the spot where you stopped your pen with a BIG NUMBER 1

4. Now from this point draw another diagonal line towards the top right hand corner but only go about half way up

5. Mark this spot where you stopped your pen with a BIG NUMBER 2

6. Draw a diagonal line from the number 2 point, parallel to the first line and down towards the bottom right hand corner. **But do not go anywhere near as far down as your number one point!** This line should be your shortest one. Make it about half the length of your number 2 line

7. Mark this point with a BIG NUMBER 3

8. Now you have a zig-zag pattern, marked clearly as a 1-2-3. Now draw a flat, horizontal line right on top of the number two point. On top of this line write: BUY HERE!!

9. Now imagine this is a stock you have been observing and it has formed a 1-2-3 bottom. If that horizontal line across the number two is taken out then you have a valid buy

10. For a 1-2-3 topping formation that gives you a valid sell signal simply reverse the whole procedure

11. Practice this fun worksheet again and again and again and then practice a little more until this pattern is firmly fixed in your mind. It takes a little time and effort to grasp the pattern

but it is like riding a bike: when you get it right, you will never have to learn it again

This is how your drawing should look (and if it looks totally different then try doing the above exercise again while looking at this drawing!):

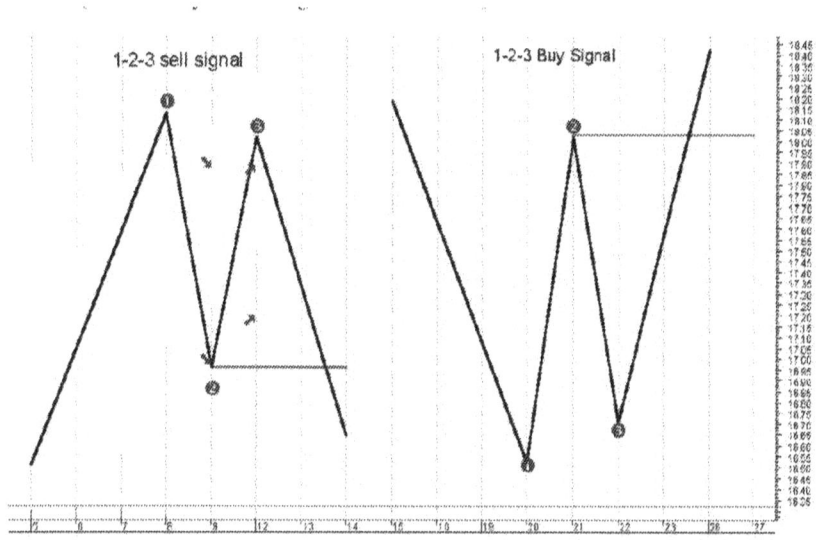

The drawing exercise is designed to get your eyes used to recognizing this 1-2-3 pattern. Have you ever had a meeting where your managers discussed doing a bunch of new things to increase sales or increase customer satisfaction and you sat there thinking, "What do they know? They just sit in their offices all day, sip coffee, and have meetings!"

Well, that is what I'm trying to avoid here. Most people tend to learn better when they are given an opportunity to do the job while learning. Haven't you ever heard of "on the job training"? Of course you have! You learn while you do. Most adult learners do it this way!

So go ahead and do some more of the exercises (as many as you need) to get that hypothetical, general feel of the pattern.

Then take a look at some more real examples:

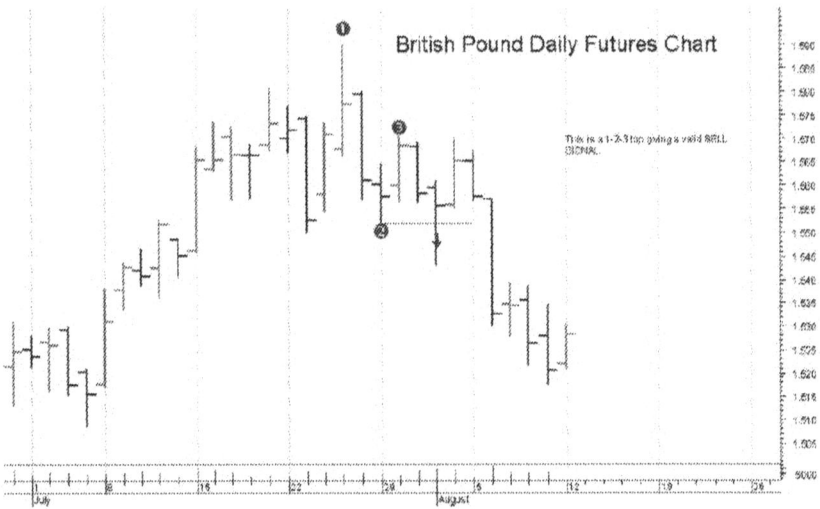

What do you notice about this chart? Can you spot how many valid 1-2-3 buy and sell signals are present on this daily bar chart of General Electric? I understand that it may be a little difficult to spot them on this shrunken down version but that is not the point. The point is that I wanted to show you just how consistent this pattern truly is. And I also wanted you to gain some confidence because I'm sure you were able to spot a few of the signals. By the way, there are twelve valid buy and sell signals on that chart!

Let's take another look from a birds eye view:

Alright. So now you can spot some valid 1-2-3 signals. So now what do you do? Practice! Practice drawing 1-2-3's (remember that fun exercise you did a little earlier?). Also practice looking for them on your favorite stocks and futures markets. They happen all the time and are about 70% accurate in the price prediction.

Now we can take a look at some different charts and time frames with 1-2-3 signals.

But before we do that, let's take one more look at what a valid 1-2-3 signal looks like on a bar chart. This one is a PERFECTLY FORMED 1-2-3 signal. Of course, we do not live in a perfect world (especially when looking at stock charts), but the idea is to get used to spotting these signals.

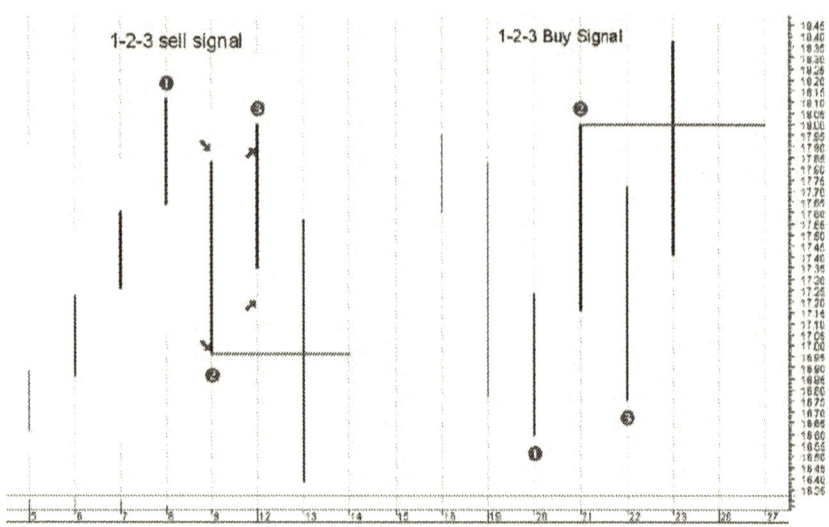

Again, the above chart represents a perfectly formed signal. Most signals will look drastically different. In fact, some signals won't even occur on the same bar. Sometimes the formations will occur over several bars and you just have to train your eye to spot the formations no matter how long, big, short, fast, low, or high it is.

Here are two examples of a 1-2-3 signal forming over multiple bars:

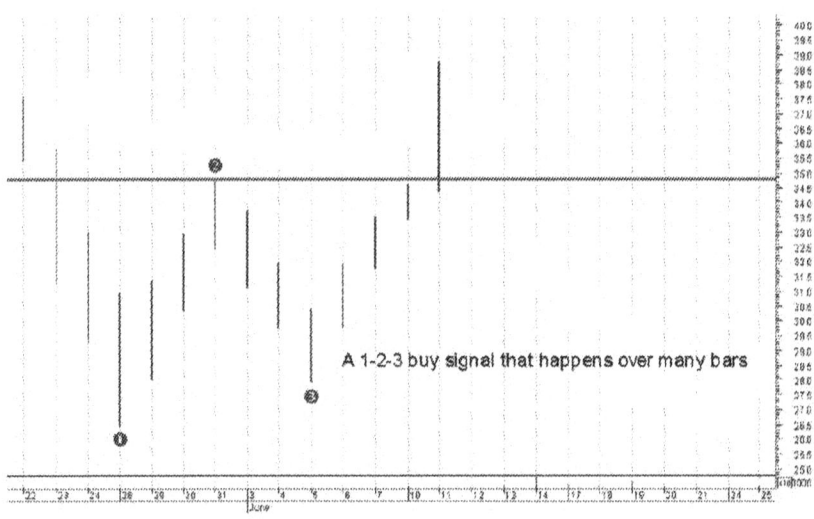

A 1-2-3 buy signal that happens over many bars

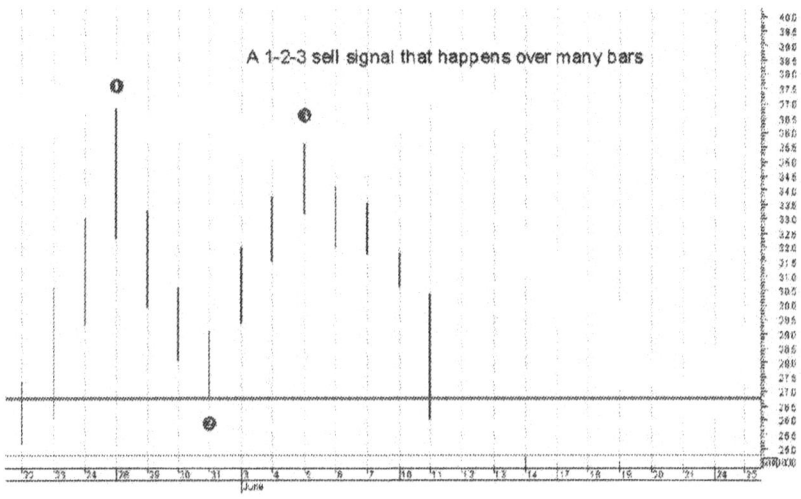

A 1-2-3 sell signal that happens over many bars

So obviously there is absolutely nothing wrong with 1-2-3 formations forming over multiple bars as opposed to the one bar corrections
shown in the perfect signal chart. And as you can see from the two
charts, 1-2-3 patterns sometimes happen very quickly and sometimes
seem to take forever to develop. All stocks are different. All markets are

different. All times are different. All economies are different. But the patterns are the same. You can pretty much bank on the patterns!

IMPORTANT POINT TO REMEMBER:

Generally, the more bars that are involved in the 1-2-3 buy or sell pattern the bigger the move. In the above three examples I would expect bigger moves from the last two charts as opposed to the first one. This is simply because there are more bars involved on those two examples. This is just a general rule, though, and nothing to live your life by. In fact, as long as you stick to your rules as stated in the first section of this book, it really won't matter how big a move it is. You will stick to your rules whether the potential payout is $10,000 or $10, right!?!

Additionally, 1-2-3 patterns happen in ALL time frames. What I mean is that you will notice these patterns whether you are looking at those five minute tick charts and you will also notice the patterns if you are looking at the yearly charts. However, since I never have and never will day trade, I will opt not to show you one of these miniscule time frame examples.

But one thing I will do is show you some weekly and monthly charts, just to prove to you that you will spot these signals no matter what time frame you are looking at. They are always valid!

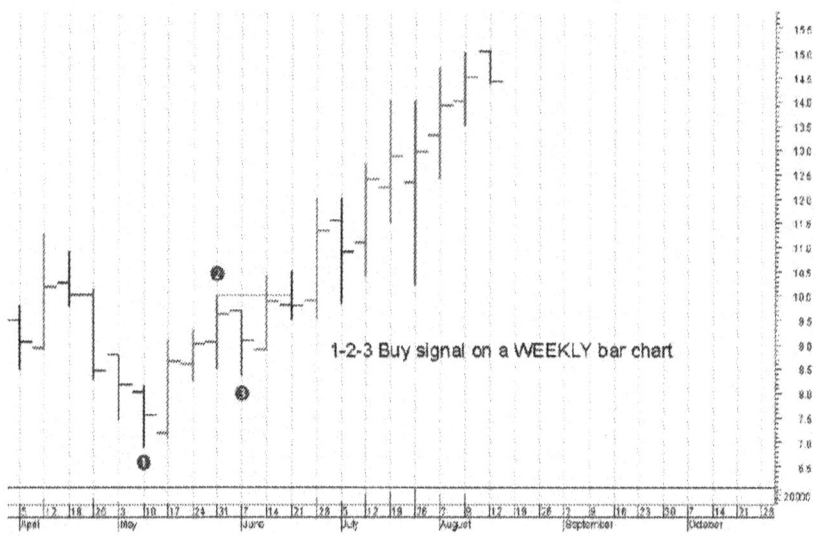

1-2-3 Buy signal on a WEEKLY bar chart

Isn't this one great! Look at that powerful 1-2-3 bottoming pattern that gave a valid buy signal at $9.80. This share happened to be at $14.50 at the time of writing. A whopping 48% gain in 10 weeks! If you had followed this simple pattern and bought where the signal told you to bought, you would have made **48%**!

Now think for a moment exactly what it takes to make these kinds of gains. Remember that this is a weekly bar chart so you could essentially have taken a look at it for a few minutes on the weekend. I mean, how long would you have had to work in order to make 48%? How long would it have taken you to spot, manage, and profit from this trade? A couple of minutes!

If this doesn't prove what a fantastic signal the 1-2-3 is then you are a tough one to please!

Now you got me excited so let's take a look at some more:

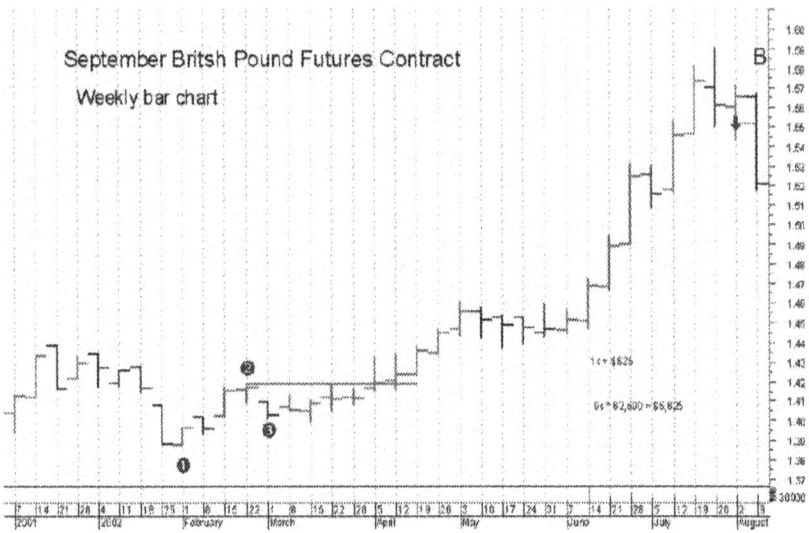

This chart is a British Pound futures contract, viewed on a weekly bar chart. Again, you'll notice the incredible up trend directly following the valid 1-2-3 buy signal (red horizontal bar at Point 2). So this is another example of a weekly chart with valid 1-2-3 signals.

So now let's look at a monthly bar chart to show you that the time frame doesn't matter…these 1-2-3 signals are everywhere!

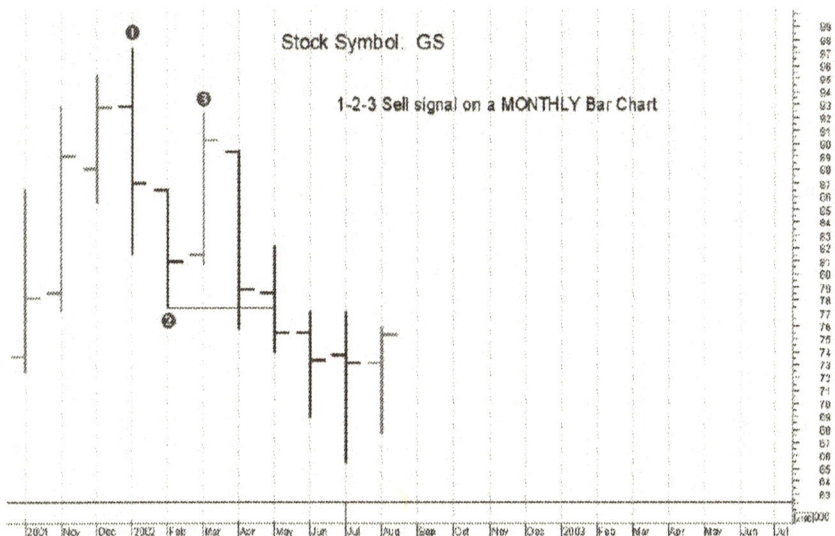

Do you remember how I had mentioned earlier that, in general, the more bars that are involved in the signal the more powerful and long lasting the move will be? Do you further remember that I had mentioned that it may not matter to you since you will be following your rules so size doesn't play a factor? Well take a look at the above chart and try and guess why size DOES matter!

Yep, you guessed it! Your rules will tell you when to get in, when to hold, and when to get out. So if you have designed your trading program to incorporate the 1-2-3 signal then your rules may tell you to expect a bigger trend with a signal on a monthly chart than you would on a weekly chart (and a bigger trend on a weekly chart than you would on a daily chart…).

Think about it: Do you think that the bigger move is going to be on a daily chart where the 1-2-3 signal develops over five bars or a monthly chart where the signal develops over ten bars? Of course you said the monthly chart!

Here is a very general rule of thumb table for you to consider: If you spot a 1-2-3 bottom on the NASDAQ monthly it could signal a new bull market that could last six months to two years (or more).

Here is a table of general move patterns. You can keep this table in the back of your mind for reference:

1-2-3 Length of Chart	Generally the Move Could Last:
daily chart	2-8 weeks
weekly chart	4-16 weeks
monthly chart	2 to 12 months

At this point you may be asking which types of charts you should be looking at in the hopes of spotting 1-2-3 signals. Well, to be very blunt...**1-2-3 patterns appear on all the charts**! Be it bars, lines, Renko, P+F, candlestick you name it. It makes no difference. The exact same pattern plays out the same.

Below is an example of a 1-2-3 signal playing out on a line chart. But let me reiterate that I am not a day trader and will not give examples of day trading. So my advice would be to look at weekly or monthly line charts when trying to spot 1-2-3 signals.

Nasdaq Composite (9216.680, 943.270, 902.260, 938.690, +1.84 930)

NASDAQ 2000 - 2002

WEEKLY LINE CHART

Again, my tip with using line charts is to use weekly or monthly only. Daily charts just give too many false signals.

But like I said, you will be able to spot these 1-2-3 signals on any chart you look at. After you practice and practice and practice some more then you will be able to spot these signals in your sleep...even if you run across a chart that you may not be totally familiar or comfortable with. So let me show you an example of a RENKO chart and see if you can spot the valid 1-2-3 signals.

Do you see them?! Can you see why using the 1-2-3 pattern on the indices on a weekly or monthly basis is one of my favorite techniques for spotting overall market trend changes? When I see a 1-2-3 bottom on a weekly or monthly chart I get very excited. If you spot one I urge you to make the VERY best investment you are likely to make. If you don't know what I mean, check out some of the resources at the end of this book (the Momentum Share Trading System that I developed will go hand in hand with the 1-2-3 signal if you use the signals to indicate market trends).

This is one of the secrets that the so-called "investment gurus" don't tell you about. You don't have to wait for them to write a newspaper article or appear on the morning news to tell you how the market is going to go. You can look at the charts yourself and trade accordingly before everyone else does (or at least at the same time as the successful traders who follow their own rules and patterns instead of waiting for a front page article in the Wall Street Journal to tell them when and what to buy).

So are you beginning to feel a little more comfortable with spotting 1-2-3 trading signals? Remember, the 1-2-3 works on:

- ALL time frames

- Both buying and selling

- Stocks

- Futures

- All types of charts (line, bar, RENKO, etc.)

You now know that if you can spot it and chart it, the 1-2-3 pattern will appear. Now let us take a look at a slight trick for entry once you have your 1-2-3 pattern firmly in place.

And try not to worry about this whole process just yet. You will develop your trading system that perfectly matches your comfort level. I'm showing you what has worked for me and how to spot the winners in the market. It's up to you to tailor this information to meet your needs as an investor. The ball will firmly be in your court!

11

Applying the 1-2-3 Trading Signal

You have now learned how to spot the 1-2-3 signal on any chart in any time frame. Earlier, I had told you to either buy or sell the breakout of the number two point. Why don't we refresh our memories and take a look at a perfect, hypothetical 1-2-3 pattern that displays a sell signal and a buy signal:

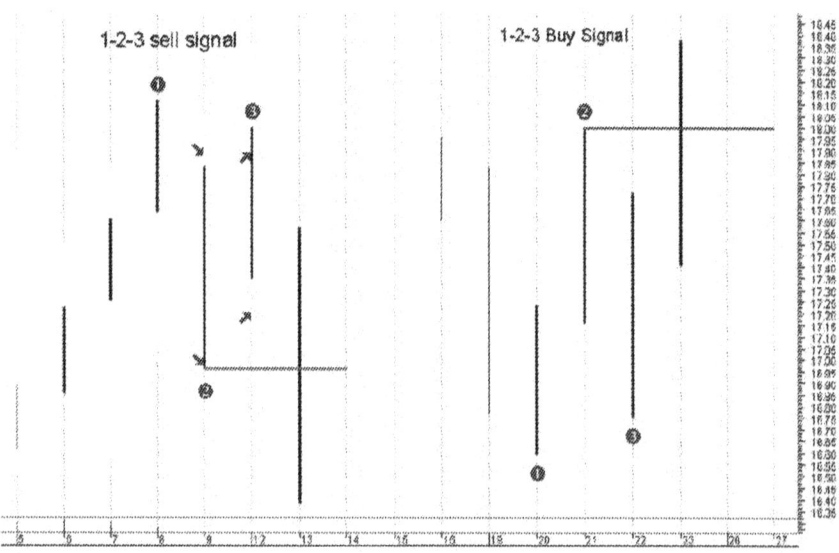

Above I simply show the valid 1-2-3 top and bottom patterns and where to place your buy/sell points. In other words, I am showing you the breakout of the number two point.

But, you see there are many traders, systems, experts, etc. that blindly sell and buy at the breakout of every pivot point on a chart. What we do know is there are usually many orders placed at the breakouts of these points (as if tons of people had their computers fixed to buy whenever there is a pivot point on the chart).

These investors have the general rule down. They are doing a fair job and are at the very least utilizing important information about the patterns of the stock market. But you can beat even this crowd (with the knowledge you have already gained, you are well ahead of the crowd that buys and sells based on the newspapers or darts). You, of course, want to be in the market just before the masses. You want to score before everyone else does. That is the game in the stock market, isn't it? But how can you achieve this?

Easy! Bring your order slightly in. Bring your order in to a buy point at a slightly lower price than the breakout of the number two point. You'll be slightly ahead of the game. Take a look:

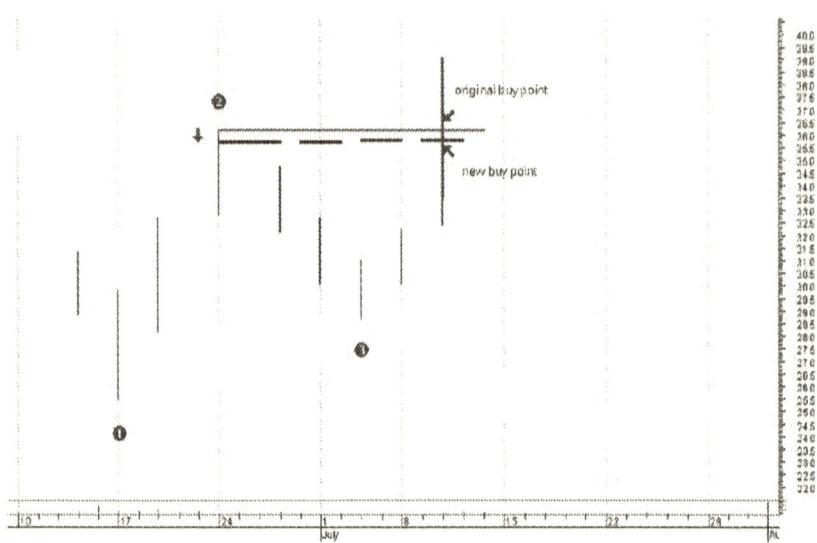

There really are no big secrets here. Instead of buying at the break-out point and joining the mass of people who have some knowledge of the game and scramble to get on board right at the breakout point, simply move your buy order in so you can enter the market slightly before most others. This will cut down on your slippage potential and will ensure that you will get a big initial move on your order (because quite a few others will be getting in slightly after you will be).

After you understand what it takes to make a successful buy, you obviously must now be in a position to make an appropriate sell. Luck-ily, the principles don't change. Take a look at the following sell order:

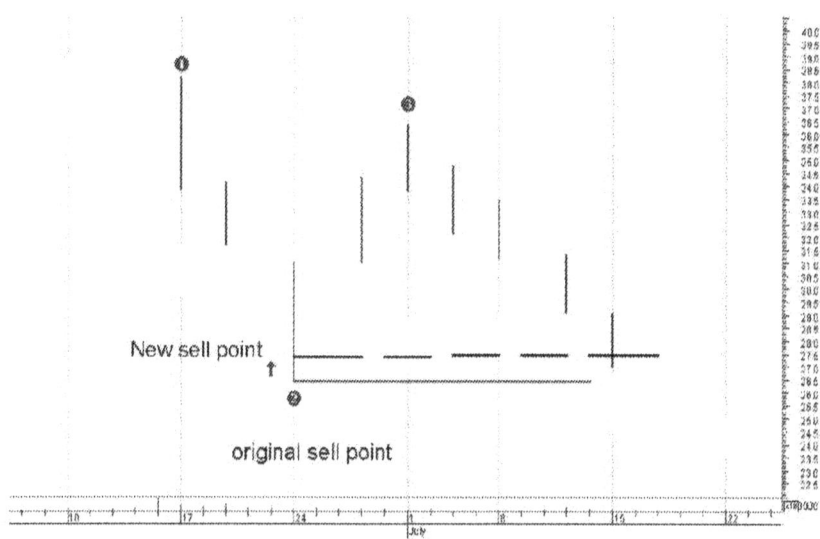

Just how far you move this buy/sell in to beat the crowd is entirely up to you, your rules, your trading ideals, and your comfort level. There is no exact scientific amount of time (or else the masses would follow it and it would keep moving back and back and back until no system would work anymore!) but you definitely want to make sure you get in with plenty of time to spare before the masses enter on the breakout.

Just keep practicing. Experiment a little to determine the numbers and times you are most comfortable with. And give a major consideration to the notion of keeping a tight (no more than 10%) initial stop loss once you have entered your trade. Again, the system that you design for yourself will reflect these rules.

Just as important as when to get into to a trade is when to get out. Now that I think about it, exiting may actually be more important than entry because this is where the money is made. Remember in Section One when I talked about trading in points rather than money? Well when you exit a trade, you are now talking about money. I always hear people talking about how much money they made or how much money they lost when a stock went up or down. Ridiculous. You don't gain or lose a penny until you sell your stock. Your buying power, your wealth does not go anywhere until you actually exit a trade. So sure, think of it as a game where you score points instead of money…but remember that the exit is where the money is truly made.

Unfortunately, a very small percentage of traders (one out of a hundred in my experience) focus as much of their attention on the exit of a trade as they do when they buy. This seems so silly because they are playing with chips and not money UNTIL THEY SELL! It is my steadfast opinion that one of the main reasons why traders fail is because they do not focus enough on the exiting of a trade. So let us take a look at some of the vital principles learned and see how they fit into my exit rules.

1. The big money is in the big moves. So when you are in a trade and it gives you some early profits, DO NOT look to bail out as soon as it starts to correct. Make it a part of your system (one of your rules) to hang in there for as long as possible and hope your small profits turn into large ones. Follow the 1-2-3 signals. If you see a signal across eight or ten bars then wait a little longer than you would if the signal were across two or three bars. You can start by using the graph I showed you earlier:

1-2-3 Length of Chart	Generally the Move Could Last:
daily chart	2-8 weeks
weekly chart	4-16 weeks
monthly chart	2 to 12 months

But remember, this is a general guideline. Once you gain enough experience you will develop your own graph to apply to your rules.

Tweak it until you can create a more accurate chart based upon your trading experiences and strategies.

2. Cut losses short. I am absolutely gob smacked when I hear of traders and investors not cutting their losses short when their rules say they should (I'm even more appalled when they don't cut their losses short AND they don't even have any rules to follow!). I'm sure you have heard it before. They may say things like, "it's not at a loss until I sell it", which is a total misunderstanding of what I was trying to say earlier. They are right that they have not yet lost money if they have not yet sold the stock. But I assure you that nobody ever made money by not selling their stock! If you don't sell, you can't make money. It's as simple as that You need to focus on the exit of the trade in order to win the game.

I have also heard things like, "but it's a good company so why should I sell?" or "if it drops any more then I will sell it". Pure insanity. These traders really need to develop some discipline and stick to their rules (of course, if they don't have any rules then they need to make some rules and *then* develop some discipline to follow those rules). The only way you can survive in the market is to cut out your losers at a pre-defined percent stop loss (as dictated by your rules). Don't second guess your system. Don't think that you should make an exception just because the company is a good company and it can't go down forever.

If your initial stop is hit then get out and move on. Don't be emotional. It's not like you will be losing a friend or a loved one. You'll be cutting a losing stock. Deal with it and move forward! Another way to think about it is to consider that the losing stock that you are holding on to for some sentimental reason may be getting in the way of you entering into a fantastic winning trade. Wouldn't it make sense to drop the loser and go looking for the winner? Again, it's all about discipline. Set up that stop loss order and don't even think about it.

3. Less is best. Most people want to actually make more trades. They like to cut off their winning stocks/futures in search of the next one. But one of the keys to making money in the markets is to actually trade less often. This means you have to be extremely patient before entering a trade and then once you are in the middle of it, it is actually much better to hold onto your winning stocks than to cut them off and initiate a new trade. The most dangerous part of any trade is when you enter, which is why most traders focus on that aspect of trading (notice I said "dangerous" not "important"). Why traders want to continue to place themselves in this danger zone more often than necessary is beyond me.

You may be thinking that number three contradicts number two. But the balance between the two is what will keep your head above water. You want to cut your losers as soon as they hit that stop loss number and you want to keep your winners so as to not risk getting rid of something good for something bad. It sounds so simple, doesn't it? Get rid of the bad stocks and keep the good ones. Yet most traders have a difficult time with these concepts.

EXIT RULES AHEAD!

So we touched on some of the basic, general guidelines to follow when creating your system. Now let's talk about what you should do once you have entered on a valid 1-2-3 pattern. First of all, you will want to set your initial stop loss relatively tight. For individual stocks I do not like to lose more than 10% of the initial investment. Find what you will be comfortable with. Futures will have to be a pre-determined dollar amount. Bear in mind, though, that a good rule to follow is that you should not be in danger of losing more than 3% of your total equity with any one trade. So if you have $10,000 in total equity and you want to know where to place a stop loss order for a new $3,000 trade I would recommend going no lower than $2,700 (so you could lose a maximum of 3% of your total equity on that one trade and a maximum of 10% of the individual trade). If your account has $20,000 then make sure each trade has a maximum risk of $600.

Of course, this is my rule. Your rules may be different. The 3/10 rule (lose no more than 3% of your total equity or 10% of the individual trade amount) seems to work in most instances because it allows for flexibility without allowing for great losses. It ensures that you can move on if you come across a loser stock.

Secondly, when you gain as much as 25% then move your stop to break even (the amount you invested plus fees). If the stock doubles back from here and takes your stop out then you have lost only your brokers transaction. In other words, once your stock has gone up by 25% then your exit will be at a place where you will neither lose nor gain any money. Sure, if your stock goes down and you reach your new exit then you left 20% profit on the table but that's the chance you took in the hope of making a much bigger profit.

Then, when you gain at least 50% you should protect half those profits until you are stopped out (if the stock has reached its peak at this point and goes back down then you will have gained 25%). Once you have gained 100% then protect 75% of those profits until you have been stopped out. Keep raising this exit marker to protect 75% of your profits until the stock finally falls back down and your rules tell you to make the exit. Most traders will have gotten out long before you have. Many would have gotten out after the 25% gain, others after the 50% gain, and yet others after the 100% gain. You'll be getting out slightly lower than the stock's peak EVERY time…and you won't even have to think about it.

Obviously, I like to keep my exits very simple and straightforward. I never rely on oscillators to tell me a market is overbought or oversold. They simply do not work. Once you have a profit it is all about hoping that profit turns into a bigger profit. And then once that profit turns into a bigger profit it is all about turning that bigger profit into an even bigger profit. You'll have to be prepared to give back a percentage of your gains in the hopes of doing this. But since you will have your specific rules in place, you really won't have to think about it at all. It will be fun because you will become excited when you are able to move to the next stop marker.

It may be easier to understand with an example so let's run through a quick scenario of stops. You have a total account worth $5,000 and you purchase $1,000 of YIC stock priced at $20. You initially set up a stop loss marker at $900 or $18 per share (no more than 10% of the one trade). Your rules then tell you to wait. Let's say that stock rises to $25. You are now at 25% profit (let's not consider fees for the moment for the sake of simplicity) so you place a stop loss order at $20 per share (up from the initial order of $18). In other words, the stock could tank at this point and you would end up getting out of the trade with neither a loss nor a gain.

Then the stock rises to $30. Now you are at 50% profit so you place a stop loss order at $25 because you are protecting half of your profits (remember, you bought at $20). Most people at this point would be getting out (if they have not already) but your simple stop loss rules tell you to stay in. Now the stock rises to $40 so you place a stop loss order at $35 (75% of the profits). If the stock were to rise any more, you would place the new stop order at 75% of the new profits. This obviously would continue until the first time the stock goes down to your exit. At this point you would just wait until your stop loss has been hit. This will ensure that you will catch any rebounds (while the last remaining bold investors have gotten out at the first site of a drop) and increase your profits even more. This will also ensure that you will end up making quite a bit from where you began.

In a nutshell, you have been given a simple exit system. Your rules will tell you what to do and when to do it. No decisions. No thought. No stress. Just think about it! You spot a 1-2-3 signal to buy a stock, you buy it, you establish your exiting strategy, you exit when your plan tells you to, and you reap the rewards of stressfree trading!

So remember, taking a profit too early is just as foolish as not cutting your losses! Just remember hope and fear.

FEAR your losses will get much bigger (so cut them off).
HOPE your profits will become much bigger (so give them the opportunity to do so).

Sadly, most do it completely the other way around. They fear that their profits will disappear so they cut them off too quickly. They hope that their losses will turn into profits so they hang onto them for far too long. Is it any wonder they lose in the markets? And although you will tailor your system to meet your needs and desires, I highly recommend you try my system first so that you can have a benchmark with which to recognize success. I've been doing this for a long time and have played with these numbers. They really work for me so utilize my experiences to your advantage. You don't have to go through nearly as much trial and error as I have gone through because you can benefit from my past successes and failures.

I started off simply following trends in stocks with sound money management rules. Guess what? I made money.

Then I embarked on a quest to find the Holy Grail of trading. I attended literally dozens of seminars and spoke with hundreds of traders. Sadly, I have bought many $3,000 (and up) black box trading systems. I purchased hundreds of books, reports, files, tapes, and CD's. You name it and I probably have bought it!

But it's almost all JUNK! Almost all of what I have bought, heard, read, and seen simply does not make money in the stock and futures markets. It's all smoke and mirrors to simply disguise the fact that I have been ripped off.

But along the way there have been a few things that I have learned:

- No man alive or system on Earth has ever, can ever, or will ever be able to predict the future market behavior. If someone tells you they can then RUN AWAY!

- Simplicity is the key. Complicated technical systems are trying to baffle you into parting with your money. If it sounds too complicated then it is probably trying to hide the fact that it doesn't work and the seller just wants your money

- Systems have three main components: 1) Trade entry/exit rules 2) Money management 3) Trader psychology

I have also learned that 95% of traders seem to want to put that last bullet point in the order of importance exactly how I have listed them (1 being the most important). However, what I have found is that the most important component of a trading system is the trader psychology. If you do not have the correct mindset then you are doomed to fail. Most traders I have come across were seeking a get-rich-quick scheme. Or they simply want to make money in the markets with no effort whatsoever by just listening to someone else's "hot tip". Then they wonder why their account is sinking faster than the Titanic. They jump into the markets with little or no stock market education but expect to compete with the most successful traders in history. Make no mistake about it. If you enter the stock market with no education then you are treating it as a gamble. Nothing more. However, if you gain an education, test, and adopt a more professional stance, then you are treating exactly as it needs to be treated: as a business. Who do you think will make more money and have less heart attacks? The gamblers or the businesspeople?

The second most important component of the trading system is the money management rules. I could trade solely on money management rules and come out delightfully ahead. I spend most of my time in this area now as a matter of fact. It's that important. I have adopted a much more businesslike approach to my trading and have seen the rewards. My gains and my life have improved dramatically as a result.

And contrary to what most investors will tell you, the least important component of the trading system is the trading system itself. I have my very simple systems now that I use like the 1-2-3 signal and they work beautifully. They may need a little tweaking here and there but I certainly don't waste my time seeking out the Holy Grail of trading…the one get-rich-quick scheme that "actually works" (if you think you know what it is, please don't tell me because I would likely scream and run in the opposite direction).

And let me reiterate that trading really is a great business…if you eliminate the stress. I used to trade from emotion and take it from me, it's not worth it! It was the most stressful time of my life. I hated it! I had no fun at all because I was constantly worried about the numbers. I was forever anxious about what might happen to my positions. I don't even want to think of where I would be right now if I continued on in this manner.

But I now apply the principles outlined in Section One of this book and make trades according to my 1-2-3 signal system and/or the Weekly Small Cap Trading System that I will talk about next chapter.

You can make your trading career as big or small as you wish. The good thing is that just because your trading career gets bigger and bigger, your ulcers don't have to follow the same path!

Just keep practicing those 1-2-3 signals and implement your stop loss rules into your trading system. Then the only one that has to worry is your broker (because it's their job to worry about everything so don't deprive them of their duties…you can just relax)!!

12

The Weekly Small Cap Trading System

The Weekly Small Cap Trading System is slightly different than the 1-2-3 system in that your main purpose is to search for the stocks that meet certain requirements. This system is actually a fun exercise for any investor whether you plan to implement it into your program or not. The reason is simple: After applying the criterion for selecting these stocks, you will begin to understand what it is you are looking for in the stock market. A lot of times I'll find investors just blindly picking stocks because of a "tip" they heard, a newspaper report, or any number of generic sources. The beauty of this program is that you can pick the stocks yourself. How do you think the investor gurus pick those stocks that you see every morning when you open the Business section of your newspaper? They follow a system. Well, believe me…it is a great deal more fun and more rewarding to pick the stocks yourself. When you just listen to someone else's advice, you really aren't trading…you are just following!

So how do you pick your stocks (other than the ways shown in the 1-2-3 signal system)? It's pretty simple. The first thing you have to do is establish some parameters. Your goal is to narrow down the field of thousands to a few dozen stocks from which to choose. Don't you think it would be a little more manageable to choose from twenty stocks instead of twenty thousand?!

The stock screener that I like best on the Internet (for sheer simplicity and usefulness) is Yahoo's. Go to their website (http://screen.yahoo.com/stocks.html) and punch in the following four parameters (you can just ignore all the others). I'll explain as I go along exactly why I set the parameters the way that I do.

SHARE DATA (stock criteria number 1):

Make the minimum share price $10.00 and the maximum share price $40.00. I really want to stress that you stay away from the penny stocks. There is absolutely no need for you to gamble away your hard earned money in these low priced stocks. Stocks under $10 can change as much as twenty to fifty percent IN ONE DAY!

"But the gains could be so huge," you might be saying to yourself. That is absolutely true...but the losses could be huge as well. And if you want to develop a trading system that can help you to become a successful, stressfree trader than you certainly don't want to be dealing with stocks that can go up or down by 50% every day. You'd be spending ten hours a day just replacing your loss stops!

And to be honest, with the superior gains you will realize by using the principles and systems outlined in this book, you will feel no need to gamble your money in the hopes of gaining 50%! After all, the smart money keeps away from those stocks...I suggest you do the same.

I also get quite a few questions on why I set the maximum share price at $40.00. The reason for this ironically is the same reason why you *don't* want to invest in anything under $10. It's just common sense. It's like the idea of diversifying your portfolio or not allowing any one trade to lose more than 3% of your portfolio. It is essentially eliminating the "unbelievable highs" as well as the "unbelievable lows".

You still can win this game by seemingly taking the middle road. But you have to have discipline. Many investors will occasionally "take a chance" only to find that if they had stuck to their original rules and goals they would have been better off financially and health wise.

So to explain the maximum…it is just much easier to catch a 200% move in a $20 stock than it is in a $60 or $80 stock. This rule is not set in stone but it is a good parameter to use just so that you don't have to worry about the "maybes". In other words, let's say that you keep sticking to your rules when all of a sudden you find yourself tempted to invest in something outside your parameters. Perhaps it was a hot tip from a friend or advice from a news columnist. Then a couple of weeks later you will see that you could have made a great deal of money had you acted on your impulse. But you stuck to your rules, didn't make the trade, and watched those that did make a lot of money.

Well I say that you would have a lot to be proud of. Sure, there will be a few times when you could have made a lot of money by not sticking to your rules. But I guarantee that there will be just as many, if not a great deal more, times that you would have lost a lot of money had you not stuck to your rules. Is it worth all the gambles? Some gamblers make it big but most lose their shirts. Why take the chance when you have the opportunity to make great trades without the stress? Remember the name of this game: Successful, **Stressfree** Trading. So make your parameters and stick to them.

So over the years I have concluded that you will catch more of the big moves in the $10 to $40 range than you can anywhere else. This system is, after all, designed to narrow the playing field. We are trying to get our weekly "stock-stalking list" to as low a number as possible. Concentrate on quality, not quantity.

AVERAGE SHARE VOLUME (stock criteria number 2):

I would really want this setting to be at 250,000 minimum but Yahoo does not go that high for a minimum. So set the floor at a minimum of 100,000 and filter those less than 250,000 out from your short list manually.

So why set such a high minimum share volume? The reason is that the less share volume there is the wilder the share fluctuations. If you notice on some of the shares that trade less than, say 50,000 per day, they are prone to large, unpredictable moves. I know I said it before that no person and no system could ever predict how the stock market will go. Well, that's just the point with this system! We want to eliminate the guesswork from the equation. I don't want to be guessing how the market is going to go or how a particular stock will perform. Guessing is just another way of saying gambling. And I'm not much of a gambler (just ask my poker buddies).

So the shares that trade less than 100,000 per day are much easier to manipulate. Floor traders and other investors love to get their hands on these shares because they can make all the difference. I don't want to spend my time worrying about shares that can be affected so easily by non-market conditions and factors. Plus these smaller shares are much more prone to gap moves so you will have absolutely no way of controlling the risk. And let's be honest, there are so many stocks out there to trade you have no reason to trade in the ones that have such high risk. Again, our point is to narrow the playing field. You want to keep cutting and cutting and cutting until you get a manageable handful of stocks from which to choose. That's the purpose of these parameters.

And why the one million shares maximum? I'm sure you have guessed it by now that the shares that trade such high volumes tend to be very large cap, high priced, slow moving stocks. We are trying to filter the best of the best. Without these parameters you might as well just throw a dart…whichever stock the dart lands on you invest in.

These parameters will give you what you want to work with.

MARKET CAPITALIZATION (stock criteria number 3):

Set the minimum at .25 billion and the maximum at 1.0 billion. But first of all let me explain what market capitalization actually means so that you can get a clear picture as to why I set these parameters the way that I do.

The market capitalization of a stock is the number of shares issued by that company times the current market value of that stock. A company that has issued 5 million shares whose shares have a current value of $15 will have a market cap of .75 billion:
5,000,000 X $15=0.75 billion or 750 million

If Company B has issued 20 million shares of stock at $20 then Company B will have a market cap of:
20,000,000 X $20=4 billion

If Company C has issued 3 million shares at $15 then Company C will have a market cap of:
3,000,000 X $15=.45 billion or 450 million

Can you tell which company is the best to invest in? Well, if you had plugged in my parameters to Yahoo's stock screener you would not even know that Company B exists because it would have been kicked out by the parameters. Which is good because even if Company B were doing quite well with their earnings and profits are looking good the stock of Company B will not likely climb as predictably or as fast as the stock for Company C.

So what makes a share price climb? That's actually a simpler question than you might think. The answer is MORE BUYERS THAN SELLERS! If there are more people out there who want to buy than there are who want to sell than the price will go up. This is simple economics. It's about supply and demand. What would happen if you placed a buy order of 1,000,000 shares for Company C? If you think that it would propel the price of Company C's stock into the stratosphere you are probably right. If Company B is a good company and other factors are favorable, that company's stock may climb as well…but at a much slower pace.

If two companies are equally well managed and have equal profit and earnings records then which company's stock will rise the fastest? The one with the smallest market cap.

But let's not get any crazy ideas of trading micro cap stocks (less than .2 billion) out of your head right now. Those are the get-rich-quick stocks. Those are the gambles. As far as I'm concerned, those stocks are equivalent to penny stocks…they are just not worth it. Of course the gains *could* be tremendous. But if something goes wrong with the stock or the market or the company then losses will not only happen very quickly they will be enormous. As you are probably beginning to realize, these parameters are designed to help you focus on trading the stocks that will help you become a successful, stressfree trader. They are not designed to help you gamble or get rich quick (you may get rich and it may be much more quickly than you imagined but that is not the focus!).

ONE YEAR STOCK PERFORMANCE (stock criteria number 4):

Plug in the parameter that the stocks had to have gained more than 100% over the year. This sounds strange but I'll explain in a minute. I know, I know…you are probably saying something like, "but if they already gained 100% over the course of the past year than how can I expect them to gain any more?"

Let me just say one thing: I never try to pick the bottoms and the tops. It's too risky and it's too much of a headache. Let the market first prove you right, then simply hop on board and ride the wave of the already established strong trend on your way to high gains. Think about it this way. Let's say you are going to the races for the day and you will be taking a bet. The bookie, in all his generosity, gives you an option:

Option One: You can either place your bet now, at the beginning of the race or…
Option Two: Without altering the odds or the payout at all, you can place your bet after the horses have completed half the race.

Which one would you place your money on? Sure, you might consider option one if you like to be stressed. But obviously most people would choose option number two. The odds of success are stacked way more in your favor. The horses that never had any chance of winning will likely fall well off the pace half way through the race. And you'll have that information! Only the strongest horses with the best riders will still be in the race half way through. Basically, you have taken away a great deal of the guesswork. The odds have been stacked massively in your favor!

As we all know the astute bookie would never give you an edge like this. That would be like the House showing you all their cards during a game of Blackjack. They would all be out of business if they gave you that advantage. It would never happen in cards or at the races.

But it does happen in the stock market. By plugging in the parameters where you want to see stocks that have at least doubled you are taking a "bet" that a strong stock that has already doubled will keep going on and on and on. What are the odds that a stock that has doubled over the course of the past year has reached its absolute peak?!

Thinking about it that way makes me wonder why anybody would risk trying to pick tops and bottoms. There's just a much easier and less stressful way to make money. Let a trend get firmly established and jump on the bandwagon. But remember, this is one of four parameters that you need to plug into the stock screener. If you just relied on this one parameter (or any single parameter) than you would probably be about 25% as successful as the rest of us following all four!

There is one more parameter that I manually plug into my screens. Yahoo does not allow for maximum price increases but I like to keep my stock picks at under 400%. So manually discard those shares that have seen a 400% gain or more over the past year.

Why? It's simply the law of averages. The more advance the stock makes, the closer it is to its peak. Sure, some stocks go on to make 1000% gains in one year but they are few and far between. Besides, we are trying to filter out the possible trouble stocks and only keep the quality stocks that have the greatest chance for success. We want to keep the risks manageable and throw out any stocks that have fallen into the HIGH risk territory.

Buy high and sell higher is the goal. But buy very high and try to sell even higher becomes too risky. Remember, these are parameters (no less than 100% and no more than 400%). The reason for not going any lower than 100% is inversely similar to the reason why you don't want to go any higher than 400%. Get the stocks in between and you'll find the winners.

So which are the stocks that we want to "stalk"? In a nutshell: We want low to medium priced, high volume, small cap stocks that have at least doubled in the past year but not gained more than 400%. Got all that?

Let's review what we **don't** want:

- penny stocks
- high priced stocks
- massively traded or non-liquid stocks
- micro-cap or anything larger than small cap stocks
- to predict moves
- to trade in stocks where the move is already (or most likely) completed

So when you get to the Yahoo stock screeners screen you will see a bunch of input options. Remember, you only need to worry about the four parameters we talked about. You will plug the numbers in like:

Stock Screener

Preset Screens
- High Volume Stocks
- Greatest Sales Revenue
- Largest Market Cap
- Strong Forecasted Growth
- 52-week Sizzlers
- 52-week Swooners

Related Resources
- SmartMoney Screens
- Mutual Fund Center
- Financial Glossary
- Co.& Fund Index
- Top Fund Performers
- Prospectus Finder
- Fund Calculators
- Education Center

Screener Settings

Search for stocks by selecting from the criteria below. Click on the "Find Stocks" button to view the results.

Category

Industry:
```
Any
Advertising (Services)
Aerospace & Defense (Capital Goods)
Air Courier (Transportation)
Airline (Transportation)
```

Index Membership   Any

Share Data

Share Price: $10   Min $40   Max

Avg Share Volume: 100k/day   Min   1m/day   Max

Market Cap: 250 mil   Min   1 bil   Max

Dividend Yield: Any   Min   Any   Max

Performance

1 Yr Stock Perf: Up more than 100%

Beta (Volatility): Any   Min   Any   Max

Sales and Profitability

Sales Revenue: Any   Min   Any   Max

Profit Margin: Any   Min   Any   Max

Valuation Ratios

Price/Earnings Ratio: Any   Min   Any   Max

Price/Book Ratio: Any   Min   Any   Max

Price/Sales Ratio: Any   Min   Any   Max

PEG Ratio: Any   Min   Any   Max

Analyst Estimates

Est. 1 Yr EPS Growth: Any

Est. 5 Yr EPS Growth: Any

Avg Analyst Rec: Any
(1=Buy, 5=Sell)

Results Display Setting

Display info for: Actively Screened   Data

Find Stocks

As you can see, there are a number of different parameters that you can plug in. But the only ones you need to worry about are the share price, average share volume, market cap, and 1 year stock performance. This filtering process will produce a list of about 15 to 20 stocks (19 in the case above…entered in on January 31, 2003). The list looks like this:

Stock Screener Search Results (Showing 1 to 19 of 19)   As of 31-Jan-2003

New Screen

Display for this screen: | Actively Screened[current] ▼ | View

Symbol	Company ▲	Retail Price	Avg. Vol	Market Cap	Return %	More Info
BSTE	Biosite Inc	35.14	556,818	520.95M	152.99	Quote, Chart, News, Profile, Reports, Research, SEC, Msgs, Insider, Financials
CCCG	CCC Information Services Group Inc	20.70	104,545	539.07M	167.10	Quote, Chart, News, Profile, Reports, Research, SEC, Msgs, Insider, Financials
CENT	Central Garden & Pet Co	21.88	134,954	413.40M	183.51	Quote, Chart, News, Profile, Reports, Research, SEC, Msgs, Insider, Financials
CHTT	Chattem Inc	15.61	235,727	287.11M	118.09	Quote, Chart, News, Profile, Reports, Research, SEC, Msgs, Insider, Financials
CQB	Chiquita Brands International Inc	14.95	311,727	585.34M	1947.94	Quote, Chart, News, Profile, Reports, Research, SEC, Msgs, Insider, Financials
DAKT	Daktronics Inc	14.77	101,272	271.00M	125.50	Quote, Chart, News, Profile, Reports, Research, SEC, Msgs, Insider, Financials
ISPH	Inspire Pharmaceuticals Inc	12.05	264,580	311.49M	241.36	Quote, Chart, News, Profile, Reports, Research, SEC, Msgs, Insider, Financials
JAH	Jarden Corp	26.20	115,090	374.95M	175.79	Quote, Chart, News, Profile, Reports, Research, Msgs, Insider
JASA	Jo-Ann Stores, Inc	25.69	161,181	500.77M	140.09	Quote, Chart, News, Profile, Reports, Research, Msgs
MVL	Marvel Enterprises Inc	11.09	471,318	673.91M	153.78	Quote, Chart, News, Profile, Reports, Research, Msgs, Insider
NTE	Nam Tai Electronics Inc	33.15	140,772	350.26M	108.23	Quote, Chart, News, Profile, Reports, Research, Insider
NTES	Netease.com Inc	14.80	547,590	449.53M	1680.49	Quote, Chart, News, Profile, Reports, Research, Msgs, Insider
NFI	Novastar Financial Inc	34.43	175,861	358.73M	108.17	Quote, Chart, News, Profile, Reports, SEC, Msgs, Insider, Financials
ODFL	Old Dominion Freight Line Inc	31.63	101,818	325.69M	131.21	Quote, Chart, News, Profile, Reports, Research, SEC, Msgs, Insider, Financials
RGLD	Royal Gold Inc	27.04	543,454	515.38M	372.73	Quote, Chart, News, Profile, Reports, Research, SEC, Msgs, Insider, Financials
SCSS	Select Comfort Corp	11.60	453,590	344.10M	246.27	Quote, Chart, News, Profile, Reports, Research, SEC, Msgs, Insider, Financials
TVX	TVX Gold Inc	15.64	175,272	674.79M	184.36	Quote, Chart, News, Profile, Reports, Research, Msgs
UNTD	United Online Inc	13.80	916,818	565.70M	190.53	Quote, Chart, News, Profile, Reports, Research, SEC, Msgs, Insider, Financials
WTEL	WilTel Communications Inc	14.98	100,272	749.00M	1088.89	Quote, Chart, News, Profile, Reports, Research, SEC, Msgs, Insider, Financials

With the above list we quickly eliminate the stocks that Yahoo couldn't filter for us. So let's get rid of those stocks with a daily volume of less than 250,000 shares traded daily. Just cross off the stocks that don't fit our pre-determined parameter. This will leave you with a much more manageable list of stocks with which to work. In this example, you would get the following list of eight stocks to work with:

1. BSTE
2. CQB
3. ISPH
4. MVL
5. NTES
6. RGLD
7. SCSS
8. UNTD

Now cross off those stocks that have gained more than 400% for the year. Remember, we have plugged in the parameter of a minimum gain of 100% for each stock but Yahoo does not allow screening of a maximum gain. So you must do this manually. Just eliminate these stocks that are in the "probably finished moving" category or the "too high risk to think about" category. This eliminates CQB (1947% gain) and NTES (1680% gain) to leave you with the following six stocks:

1. BSTE
2. ISPH
3. MVL
4. RGLD
5. SCSS
6. UNTD

No questions. No analyzing. Just simple elimination of the stocks that don't fit into the parameters that you have pre-set. No stress!

Even if the stock criteria fails by just one percent or one volume, delete it. We want to take all the guesswork out of choosing stocks. You have to stick to your rules and your filtering process NO MAT-TER WHAT! Don't worry, you will always have enough stocks to work with. We are trying to be as selective as we can be.

And also remember that one or two big moves in the market is bet-ter than taking dozens of smaller trades.

Now take a quick look at some of the gems that we now have left from our weekly stock selection. Out of some 20,000 stocks out there we are left with these stocks:

SYMBOL	PRICE	AVERAGE VOLUME	MARKET CAP	YEARLY ADVANCE
BSTE	$35.14	556,818	520.95M	152.99%
ISPH	$12.05	264,590	311.49M	241.36%
MVL	$11.09	471,318	673.91M	153.78%
RGLD	$27.04	543,454	515.38M	372.73%
SCSS	$11.60	453,590	344.1M	246.27%
UNTD	$13.80	916,818	565.7M	190.53%

Talk about small cap gems that the market already clearly loves! Now we must find out how to trade them to make maximum profits. You could certainly just set entry and exit parameters to your trades of these stocks in much the same way as you would with the 1-2-3 signal system. But let's talk about an entry and exit strategy that may be bet-ter suited for this small cap trading system.

First let's take a look at a bar graph of a stock that recently fit our four criteria and that we received from Yahoo's screening page.

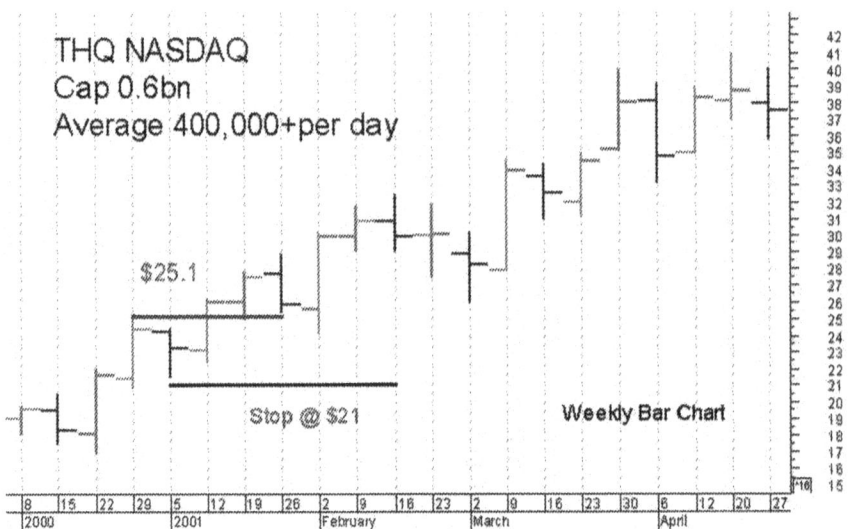

The entry position for this stock is simple to spot. Just wait for a correction on the weekly bar chart and place a buy stop a fraction above the break out ($25.1 on the above example). The point is to buy on the way up so you'll know where to appropriately place your exit. When you see peaks and valleys, buy when it reaches slightly beyond the previous peak as it's recovering from its last valley.

The initial stop is not going to be a simple, mechanical percentage stop. Instead, place the initial stop a fraction below the low after the break out bar (at $21 on the above example). This initial stop is $4.1 below the buy order...or a whopping 16%. You've already chosen the stock so the hard part is over. You have already identified the winners so now just buy in at the previous peak and put a stop at the previous valley. This exit order is rather important. Let me explain.

You must place the stop here, rather than say at a mechanical 5% or 10% below the buy order because occasionally the stock will retest this low point. Most investors who place their stops via percentages will miss out on any rebounds that the stock may have. Have you ever traded on Ebay? It kind of works the same way. When an item is listed at $10 and you need to input your maximum bid, you may be tempted to place that maximum bid on a nice round number. But the smart bidders will place that maximum bid a couple pennies ABOVE their maximum so as to weed out those that placed their bids at the nice round number. Get it? In other words, if your maximum bid is going to be $15 for the item then you would want to tell Ebay that your maximum bid will be $15.19 or something like that in order to beat those bidders who put their bids at $15 or $15.01…

So it's the same with you initial stop order. Place it slightly below what many investors would. If the stock retests this low, then you don't want to be out like many investors.

However, these will be your rules so if the stop is too big for your liking then either reduce the amount of capital you trade with or simply pass on this trade. Fit this rule into your system. But do not compromise the stop simply to trade with a tighter stop loss (i.e. with a smaller percentage of possible loss…this system really shines when you follow these rules). It will mean that you will take too many unnecessary small losses. And don't you hate when you lose an Ebay bid and you find out that the winner beat you by seven cents!?!

Let's take a look at a positive situation that you will find yourself in that sometimes leaves investors questioning what they should do. We'll use the same stock (THQ) that we used in the previous example. Let's say that you bought in at $25.1 like in the previous example and you placed your stop loss at $21. Now the stock begins to rise. Obviously, there is going to come a point where you will want to change your stop losses. But there may also come a point where your rules will tell you to re-buy this stock. That's great! Follow your rules even if your emotions are telling you, "I just bought this stock two weeks ago at $25 and now my rules are telling me to buy more of it at $32? That's crazy, I should have just bought more shares at $25!"

That thinking is all well and good but most of us cannot predict the future (by the way, if anyone can predict the future can you tell me whether or not the Cubs will go to the World Series in my lifetime because I want to be able to prepare for the occasion!). So if your rules tell you to buy you need to buy…regardless of what your emotions tell you. By now you shouldn't even be thinking about it!

Let's take a look at the example:

Pyramiding Into The Position:

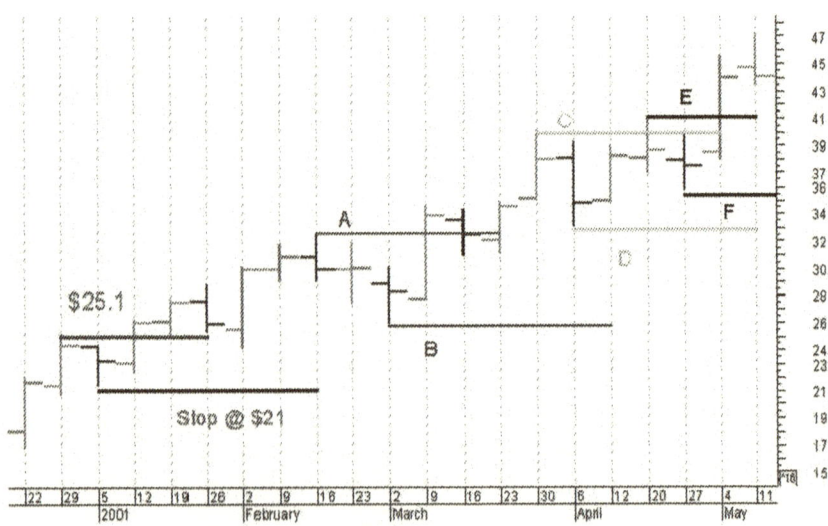

Notice the adding of positions at break outs and moving of the stop loss behind the low AFTER the break out. You are going to want to buy in again at Point A and then move the stop loss up to Point B after the low point has been established.

As time goes on you begin to notice the same pattern, only a little higher up the chart. This is great! Simply buy in again at Point C. The stop loss stays way down at Point B until Point C is established (a low after a break out). Then move your stop loss up to Point D. These moves should be automatic and without hesitation...regardless of the fact that you already own this stock!

Remember, each trade needs to be treated as unique. You'll need to apply your rules to each trade **all the way through to the end**. It makes no difference what has happened in the past.

One thing you may want to do, however, is to establish a rule for how many times you are going to buy into the same stock. I never buy into the same stock more than three times but you can do whatever is comfortable for you...until you are completely stopped out of the trades. For instance, take a look at what happened to this stock. You did quite well but when it is time to end, it is time to end!

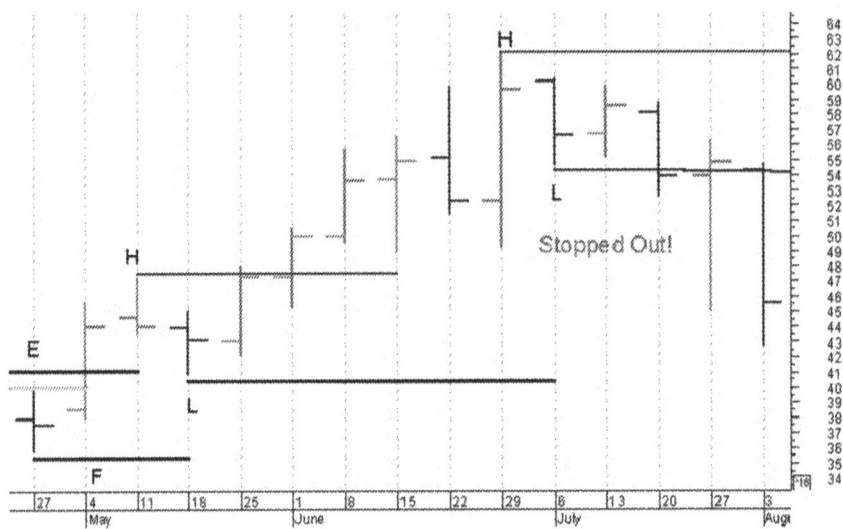

So what does it take to trade using the Weekly Small Cap Trading System?

- About ten minutes a week

- 100% objectivity (no emotion, no re-considerations)

And that's about it! This system follows a very simple procedure for finding those small cap, momentum gems. And the great thing is that the market has already told you which stocks are the winners. You just have to tag along for the ride!

And the reward/risk ratio is really the best that I have ever seen with any trading/filtering system. Besides the financial rewards that you will reap, you will also gain a great deal of confidence in the fact that you won't have to listen to anybody else tell you which stocks to trade. You can pick your own! And you won't get stressed by your decisions because you will be following your pre-determined set of rules. You'll simply cross off the stocks that don't meet your criteria and keep the ones that do. It's that easy!

Let's take a look at a total trade…one that you would see using the Weekly Small Cap Trading System.

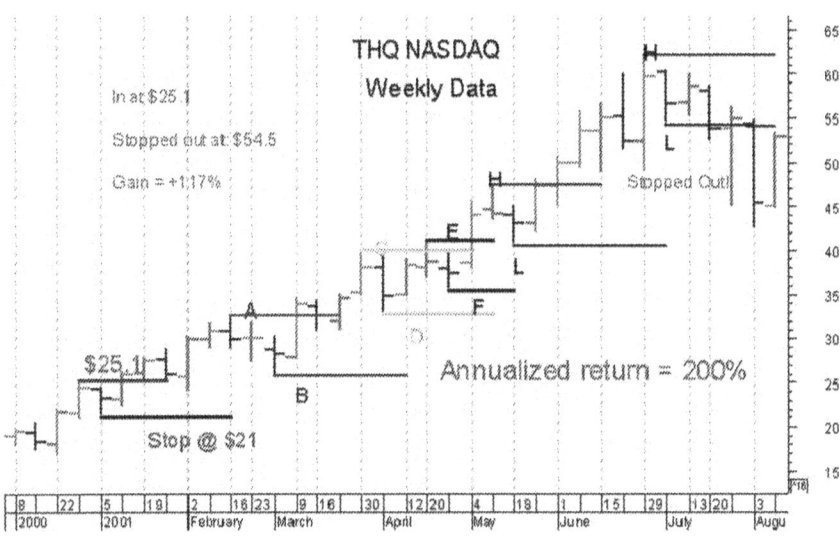

What do you notice most about this complete trade? The entries, the exits, the stops, the patterns? Nah, we all notice THE RETURN!!

So take this system and mold it to fit your needs and wants as a trader. Make it your own. Set your rules. You can even combine aspects of this system with the 1-2-3 signal system to create the Laurie-andBobSmith trading system!

The Weekly Small Cap Trading System is all about narrowing the field to find the market gems. Then you have to have an entry and exit system to follow so that you don't have to put any thought into the decisions. If your field has been narrowed to six stocks and your rules tell you to buy just above the break point on each stock's bar graph then do it! You may only see that break point or entry point on two of those six stocks. That's fine! Remember, quality...not quantity.

Just make sure you follow your rules...and trade without stress!!

Conclusion

After finishing this book, I returned to Maria's class with a sense of accomplishment because the thoughts that went into the information for this book were thoughts that I had had throughout the entire Applied Behavioral Science program. They were so much a part of my studies and my participation in the class that once the book was completed I wasn't sure if I would know how to continue with the classes. What would my motivations be?

But as always, Maria immediately put things into perspective as soon as I entered the class for the first time after completing the book. And I doubt she had any idea that she was having such an impact!

The other students and I entered the classroom to find a bunch of old mirrors lying on the table in the front of the room. They were all different. Some of the mirrors had cracks in them, some were faded, some were dirty, some were new, etc. Since it had always been great fun for us to figure out what exactly Maria was trying to do before she did it, we immediately began talking about the mirrors.

One of the students offered the suggestion that Maria was going to get superstitious and start talking about bad luck. Another thought she might talk about the different perceptions that we have of ourselves...how we look at ourselves. Believe me, there were plenty of explanations to go around!

But when Maria walked in the room, she started labeling the mirrors by affixing big letters on each one (the cracked mirror had the letter 'A', the dirty mirror had the letter 'B' and so on and so forth). She then asked us to systematically walk in a line and look into each mirror. We were told to write down what we saw in each mirror.

What I saw in each mirror was pretty predictable. In the mirror that had a big crack in it, I saw my face with a big crack down the center of it. In the dirty mirror I saw a cloudy portrait of myself. In the clear mirror I saw a perfect reflection of my face.

After we were all finished reflecting (get it?), Maria went to the blackboard and wrote: Cliché—good communication requires a good speaker and a good listener. We had all heard that before (and most of us at one point or another had tried to use that on our spouses during "discussions") but the exercise with the mirrors really drove the point home and illustrated just what that old cliché really means. When we looked in the dirty mirror (the speaker), we (the listeners) saw a shady reflection of ourselves. Now was that the mirror's fault or was that our fault? Does it matter whose fault it is? Of course not! The point is that the message got scrambled a little bit on its way from the speaker to the listener. Something had to be done. Figuring out who's fault it was would have been a big waste of time.

As a result of that class, I began to think about this book and the messages contained within. Certainly if you did not get the messages there was some problem with the communication method! The words I used in this book were designed to help you understand what it means to be a successful and stressfree trader. These words were meant to guide you in your own discoveries as an investor.

But these aren't just words. To quote Joseph DeVito, author of the *Interpersonal Communication Reader* (2002, pg. 9): Words are tools which people use to give and get information. So I'd like to emphasize the meaning of *his* words…you've been given tools. Tools that (I hope) will give you the information necessary to become a successful and stressfree trader. How you choose to use these tools is entirely up to you. But should it stop here? No way!

Keep learning. Keep asking questions. Keep trying to understand exactly who you are as an investor. But make sure that you know how to ask questions and accept feedback! If you are stuck or you think you need a little more information in order to make a trade, go ahead and ask someone who knows. But be ready for the answer and use it accordingly! When you decide to ask questions in order to get more of the information that you need, you need to be "prepared to listen attentively to the responses they provoke…or risk finding yourself worse off than ever" (DeVito, pg. 64).

And if you think you got a cracked or smudged book and the message is just not getting through clearly, don't worry! We have made plenty so you can buy as many copies as necessary before finding the one that gives you clarity!

Happy investing!!

References

Boyle, William (1999). *Getting Connected: How to Improve All Your Relationships*. William Boyle and Associates, Elk Grove Village.

Covey, Stephen (1990). *The Seven Habits of Highly Effective People*. Simon & Schuster, New York.

Darvas, Nicolas (1986). *How I Made $2,000,000 in the Stock Market*. Lyle Stuart Publishing, New York.

DeVito, Joseph (2002). *The Interpersonal Communication Reader*. Allyn & Bacon, Boston.

Hamilton, Cheryl with Parker, Cordell (1997). *Communicating for Results: A Guide for Business & the Professions*. Wadsworth Publishing Company, New York.

Hersey, Paul; Blanchard, Kenneth H.; Johnson, Dewey E. (2001). *Management of Organizational Behavior: Leading Human Resources*. Prentice Hall Publishing, Upper Saddle River.

Hill, Napoleon (1996). *Grow Rich! With Peace of Mind*. Fawcett Books, New York.

Keirsey, David and Bates, Marilyn (1984). *Please Understand Me: Character & Temperament Types*. Gnosology Books, Ltd., Del Mar.

0-595-27505-2